I0520776

The Fire Within

Awaken Your Inner Gifts to Turn Burnout and Uncertainty into Breakthrough

A Weekend Guide to Your Next Chapter

Henry C. Shelton, Jr.

ISBN: 979-8-9939318-0-7

DEDICATION

For every awakened soul who knows deep down that there is more to life than merely making a living.

ACKNOWLEDGEMENTS

I would like to thank my family for being a constant source of inspiration, encouragement, and support. First to my parents, Berneice and Henry Sr., for setting an example of the importance of reading for my siblings, Pamela, late brother Vincent Sr., and me.

To my wife, Vanessa, for establishing and maintaining an atmosphere of love, support, peace, patience, and harmony during the writing of the book, as well as transcribing my initial thoughts and words into the first draft sixteen years ago! To my son and grandson, Malachi and Sean, for being constant reminders of the book's message: discovering our inner gifts. To my daughter Imisha for reminding me of the importance to others of the assessment instrument accompanying the book. I want each of you to know that the many birthday dinners, the many trips, national and international, have all contributed to me gaining a holistic perspective on the importance of individuals coming into, discovering, and living from their own birth gifts. Not to mention that you guys are just a fun bunch to hang out with.

A special word of gratitude to my book coach, Dr. Carey Yazeed, for putting the crazy idea in my head in mid-July, that 'I could write a book in 7 days'…and 'be holding a published book in my hand by Christmas'; and then helping to make it happen! And last but not least, to the teachings of the Rosicrucian Order, AMORC, my early church days, and to the God of my heart for the spiritual guidance underlying my work.

PROLOGUE

I wrote **The Fire Within** for mid-life professionals who have reached the height of career success yet still feel an emptiness inside; some of which are rather afraid amidst these uncertain times, the ones asking quietly, *"Is there more to life than simply making a living? What's next?"* These individuals perhaps have reached a point of burnout and are now looking for a way out of their current situation. I know this dilemma all too well, as I myself experienced it at the peak of my career in Corporate America. My own journey took me from the corporate grind to the quiet chambers of Egypt's pyramids, where I encountered the wisdom of the Neteru and the language of archetypes. I was also inspired by Stephen Covey; after modeling my corporate life around his Seven Habits of Highly Effective People when in his sequel to that book, The 8th Habit, he suggested that the next step to becoming effective was to find greatness. In this he suggested that the path to greatness was to find our "voice" and then help others find theirs. This became a mantra for me, and indeed the guiding motive for the next phase of my life! These experiences convinced me of one thing: real security doesn't come from careers, titles or paychecks, but from awakening and activating the **hidden gifts you were born with.** This book is an invitation to rediscover your authentic self, awaken your innate potential, and step beyond burnout and uncertainty into a life and enterprise aligned with your deepest purpose and destiny. It's about finding your own "voice" awaiting to be discovered from the depths of the fire within.

CONTENTS

INTRODUCTION
THE WAKE-UP CALL

You can feel it.

The creeping unease, the discontent, the frustration, exhaustion, disappointment, the quiet disillusionment, the sense that despite all you've achieved, something essential is missing. On paper, you've built the life that others admire, the career, perhaps the income, the seemingly, perceived stability. Yet inside, there's a restlessness you can't ignore.

This book is about that restlessness. It's about the moment when corporate success no longer feels like true success, and when burnout and uncertainty begin to whisper a deeper truth: ***you were made for more***.

That whisper often builds quietly until, one day, it becomes unmistakable—an *Aha Moment!*

An **Aha Moment** is more than a flash of insight; it's a

sacred turning point where something deep within you clicks into alignment. It's the moment when scattered ideas, forgotten dreams, and soul whispers converge, giving you sudden clarity about who you are and why you're here. It may arrive like an epiphany or a eureka moment, but its essence is always the same: truth revealing itself.

Later in this book, as we explore finding your life purpose and awakening the courage to live it, we'll see how your Aha Moment becomes the golden thread connecting your pain, your passion, your gifts, and the people you're meant to serve. Declaring it is an act of power; it shifts you from passive reflection to intentional creation. When you name it, you claim it. You're no longer waiting for life to show you what's next; you're stepping forward with purpose.

I know this because I've lived it. For decades I worked in Corporate America, excelling in fields from biomedical engineering, installing some of the very first Magnetic Resonance Imaging (MRI) and Positron Emission Tomographic (PET) scanners in the U.S., to building a thriving Information Technology (IT) and technical training business. On the outside, it looked like success. Inside, I was unfulfilled, even sick from the stress of working for visions that sometimes weren't my own.

Throughout this time, I faced personal losses (divorce, deaths, etc.) that forced me to question everything; my career, my beliefs, even the meaning of life itself. This led me on a search beyond corporate ladders and boardrooms into the study of metaphysics and mysticism. Eventually, it carried me across the ocean to Egypt, where visitations to many ancient temples, culminating in an initiation in the King's Chamber of the Great Pyramid changed my perspective forever. Immersed in the wisdom of the Neteru, I encountered the symbolic language, a language hidden for thousands of years that gave clarity to the ancient Egyptians. This encounter of what was called Gods and Goddesses, was later revealed to be inner aspects of nature, or what the ancients referred to as Neters. Over time I would, using the wisdom of Carl G. Jung to correlate and transpose these Neters to what is known as Archetypes, timeless principles that revealed the **inner gifts** hidden within each of us.

Upon my return to the United States after my trip to Egypt in 2011, the overarching question on my mind that I was seeking the answer to became clear to me after a few years of research and study. Finding the answer to this question has since become the basis for the foundation of my life's work. It is indeed the source material for the "Accessing Your

Archetypes" assessment instrument that I created to assist others with embarking on an allegorical journey of inner introspection without having to travel to Egypt or spend years like me   discovering the connection and correlation between those ancient symbols and their significance to finding one's own calling, destiny, or life purpose.

During my visit to the many ancient temples of Egypt, most of which date back some three to five thousand years; I became overwhelmed after about a week of gazing at the thousands of hieroglyphic inscriptions ("meduNeters" or "sacred writings") engraved on the walls of the many temples, steles and pyramid walls.   All of these were inscribed with artisan-like precision and detail. After seeing these over and over repeatedly throughout that country, knowing full well that this level of work took countless hours, days and years to complete, the overarching question in my mind was this: *"To what end did the beings who did this live to?"* For clearly, they lived to a different end than what we witness today in our global society.

But even as I embraced this spiritual awakening, I wrestled with a practical question: *What was my true purpose in life to be?* Could I remain a technical engineer and IT manager and entrepreneur by day, while living as a heart-centered instructor and mentor by night?

That tension pushed me into a new path. Over time, I trained more than five hundred managers and entrepreneurs through a multi-year contract with the State of Texas. I then launched my own coaching practice to help others navigate the same crossroads I had faced.

What I discovered; and what you will discover in these pages, is that your real security has never come from your employer, your title, or your paycheck. It comes from your **divine birth gifts, discovering your calling—your unique "soul's code."** These inner gifts are the fire within. When you wake them up and activate them, burnout becomes breakthrough, uncertainty becomes clarity, and the corporate grind becomes a launching pad for a purpose-driven life and enterprise that ignites your heart-centered passion within!

This book is a weekend guide for that awakening. By the time you finish, you'll see clearly that everything you need to step into your next chapter (clarity, confidence, and courage) is already within you.

It's time to stop asking *"What's next?"* and begin declaring: *"This is who I am. This is what I was born to do."*

Welcome to *The Fire Within.*

1

THE FIRE WITHIN

"I am sick and tired of being sick and tired." — Fannie Lou Hamer

Fannie Lou Hamer spoke these words during the Civil Rights Movement, not as a slogan but as a cry from within. Born the youngest of twenty children to sharecroppers in Mississippi, she endured poverty, violence, and systemic oppression. She joined the fight for voting rights and discovered her gift for rallying voices. Her speeches moved crowds not because she was polished, but because she spoke from her heart and authentic voice. When she said she was "sick and tired," it was not a complaint; it was clarity. That inner strength carried her through beatings, jailings, and rejection — all intended to silence her voice — yet she refused to bow. Her journey reminds us that silence takes many forms — sometimes it is imposed by systems meant to suppress, and other times it comes as self-inflicted, such as when our own inner voice has been unheard for too long.

The late writer and poet Maya Angelou understood silence in a different way. She was eight years old when she stopped speaking after a traumatic event, where she thought her voice had caused her abuser to be killed. She literally thought that her words had the power to kill, so she chose silence. People mistook her quiet for brokenness. Yet in that silence, she devoured books, memorized poetry, and listened to the music of words. When her voice returned nearly five years later, it carried the fire of wisdom, rhythm, and truth that would inspire millions. Her silence had not extinguished her fire; it had strengthened it.

You may not have endured years without words like Angelou or systemic violence like Hamer, but perhaps you've endured years without your true voice. That ends today, as this book was written to help you find it again. Corporate titles, steady paychecks, long commutes, and endless deadlines can muffle the deeper sound of your soul. Burnout is not proof your fire is gone; it's proof that your fire is waiting to be heard again.

This is the essence of the fire within: the spark of your innate gifts. They manifest as the courage of the Warrior, the oration of the Scholar, the wisdom of the Sage, the aesthetics and cheer of the Artisan, the vision of the Seer, and many more. You were born with them, and they have never left you. Burnout happens not when the fire dies, but when we drift too far from it.

The Soul's Spark

Within each of us is an element of cosmic fire; that part of us connected to the divine source. Some call it God, others the Holy Spirit, Allah, Jehovah, the Cosmic Mind, or universal consciousness. Regardless of the name, most agree there is such a source. It is the primordial essence of our eternal being, the soul-self that animates us.

This essence is constructive and creative in nature. It is always moving, always creating, always evolving. Because you are connected to it, you too are by nature a creator. As children, we know this instinctively. We imagine freely, create without fear, and live in blissful alignment with our gifts.

I remember the sparks of this in my own childhood.

- **At pre-school**, I'd race to the chalkboard, eager to be the first to demonstrate my ability to write the alphabet. Something in me lit up when I had the chance to demonstrate, to show, to express.

- **In church**, I was always eager to do the verbal review of our Sunday School lesson. My chest swelled as the congregation applauded. I didn't yet know it, but I was discovering that my words could move people. I recall one of the church ministers telling my mom, "This child is going to be either a teacher or preacher".

- **On my grandfather's farm**, I marveled at seeds becoming watermelons and strawberries. Later, I started my own garden. Every sprout whispered a lesson: nurture brings harvest. I loved it when my mom used the vegetables from my garden to make parts of our dinner!

- **Through art**, I spent hours sketching cartoons. I would watch James McGill; an older friend in my neighborhood and subsequently learned from him. I remember winning art contest in elementary school with my gift. I also remember friends and family commenting to my mom on my amazing skill at drawing. I loved to hear those compliments.

These weren't hobbies, they were signals. Glimpses of the

fire within that would later become my calling as a coach, teacher, and builder of enterprises.

Personal Significance

Beneath every pursuit of success lies a deeper yearning, the desire to know that our lives matter. This is the search for *Personal Significance*, the quiet realization that your worth has never depended on performance or praise. It is the awareness that you are valuable because something sacred lives within you, a divine essence that no title, paycheck, or position can define.

Personal Significance is not about ego or comparison; it is about essence. It is the remembrance that you were created with purpose and that your gifts are divine instruments waiting to be expressed. When you reconnect with this truth, burnout loses its grip, and the fire within steadies into strength and clarity.

As you begin to see yourself as significant, not for what you do but for who you are, you start to move through the world differently. You stop striving to prove your worth and begin living from it. Purpose flows naturally from this awareness. When you honor your own significance, you awaken the confidence to serve others from authenticity, not obligation.

This inner recognition becomes the foundation for your *true calling.* When you know that your life already matters, your service becomes not an attempt to gain meaning but an expression of the meaning that has always been there.

When you live from this awareness of inner worth, your thoughts begin to change. You start to see them not as random ideas but as living seeds of creation.

Thoughts Are Things

As children, we create without judgment. My son Malachi once handed me an imaginary cup of cocoa when he was three years old. He was so convinced of its reality that he insisted that I lift it to my lips and take a sip. He paused to see my response to his freshly whipped cup of hot cocoa! I had no choice but to give him a response. To him, the cocoa in his mind was real! Because it was real! This is how we must treat our inner fire as adults.

Every creation begins twice: once in the mind, then in the physical world. A thought is not just a fleeting idea; it is the seed of manifestation. When our thoughts align with the constructive nature of divine creation, they gain the power to become real.

That's why when we search for purpose, the answer cannot come only from outside voices. It must be born in the quiet conviction of our own mind and soul. Consequently, it is within the fire of the soul that we discover the inner gifts that inspire us in finding our life purpose.

Recognizing your own significance naturally awakens a desire to serve. Once you know that your life already carries meaning, you begin to look for ways to extend that meaning into the world.

Awakening to Service

When you reconnect with your fire, it naturally points toward service. The needs of the world are endless, but not all are yours to meet. The spark within you will guide you to the particular need your soul is drawn to address.

This is where Fannie Lou Hamer's story echoes so powerfully. She didn't set out to be a civil rights leader. She was born with the inner gift of *justice*! She simply answered "the fire within" her to speak against injustice. That fire became her compass, and her voice became a catalyst for the civil rights movement.

The same is true for you. Your role is not to fix the entire world, but to align your birth gifts with the piece of the world that most needs them. That alignment is your calling.

Reflection: Finding Your Fire

To begin reconnecting with your fire within, take time away from distraction and ask yourself:

- What brings me the most joy when I'm doing it?

- What do I do with little effort, that doesn't feel like work?

- What needs of the world move me deeply, stirring something in my conscience?

Write your answers. Sit in silence and let them expand. The fire within will not shout — it whispers. But once you hear it, you will not forget it.

Closing

When we listen to the fire within, we move from insignificance to significance, from burnout to breakthrough. We inspire others simply by becoming who we truly are. When we do, we contribute to the tipping point of human consciousness, the moment when individual sparks ignite into collective light.

Your fire is not waiting to be given by a job, a paycheck, or a title. It is already yours. Angelou found hers in silence. Hamer found hers in struggle. I found mine in childhood sparks that never left. You will find yours too.

In the next chapter, we'll see how the very problems that weigh you down may actually be invitations, thresholds, or opportunities, calling you into your next chapter.

2

PROBLEMS ARE INVITATIONS

"The dogmas of the quiet past are inadequate to the stormy present. The occasion is piled high with difficulty, and we must rise with the occasion.
As our case is new, so we must think anew, and act anew."

— *Abraham Lincoln, December 1, 1862*

Lincoln's words, spoken over 163 years ago, at one of the most turbulent moments in American history, capture the essence of transformation. He understood that the old ways of thinking could not solve new challenges; that when the world shifts, so must we. His timeless call to "think anew, and act anew" is as relevant today as it was then.

In the midst of America's darkest hour, President Abraham

Lincoln told Congress that the assumptions of the past could no longer carry the weight of the stormy present. He reminded them that circumstances had changed so dramatically that they demanded new thinking and new action. His words were not only for his time; they are timeless. They echo across centuries as a call to every generation facing turbulence and transition.

Scripture echoes this wisdom: "Neither do men put new wine into old wineskins: else the wineskins burst, and the wine is spilled, and the skins perish: but they put new wine into fresh wineskins, and both are preserved" (Matthew 9:17, ASV).

Both Lincoln and the Bible remind us that old vessels cannot hold new wine. Problems arise when the life you have built can no longer contain the greater life pressing to emerge. The discomfort you feel is not punishment; it is preparation. It signals that something larger, something more significant, is trying to be born. Pain, then, is not a curse. It is a signal that life is insisting you grow into new paradigms capable of carrying your greatness and significance.

When we attempt to solve new challenges with old paradigms, we experience frustration, futility, and even despair. It is like pouring new wine into old vessels; the container cannot hold what is emerging. This is why so many feel stuck. The structures, mindsets, and habits that once worked become brittle when life calls us to step into a greater dimension of who we are.

The turbulence you feel may simply be life refusing to let you settle for less than your greatness. Problems are invitations to rise into significance, to align with a new paradigm of purpose. The old patterns: survival, stagnation, or even outward success without fulfillment, cannot contain the fullness of your calling.

When you recognize this, the dark season no longer appears as an enemy but as a midwife. It is delivering you into something greater, urging you to become a new vessel capable of carrying new wine.

From Problem to Purpose

Jack Ma applied for thirty jobs and was rejected by all of them.

KFC came to China, hired twenty-three out of twenty-four applicants, and turned him away. Harvard rejected him ten times. He often jokes that failure was his constant companion. Yet in those repeated disappointments, Ma saw something else: opportunity. He noticed how difficult it was for Chinese merchants to connect with global markets. What looked like rejection after rejection became the seed of Alibaba; China's version of Amazon.com, one of the most successful e-commerce companies on earth. Jack Ma went from serial failure to founding a company whose American initial public offering (IPO) on the New York Stock Exchange in 2014 raised US$25 billion, giving the company a market value of US $231 billion and, by far, then the largest IPO in world history.

Perhaps you yourself have experienced failures. Maybe you were passed over for a promotion, downsized in a wave of layoffs, or quietly disillusioned by a career that promised meaning but delivered monotony. It's important for you to understand that these are not dead ends. They are thresholds. The problems that frustrate you most; broken workplaces, meaningless tasks, wasted potential, may be the very invitations your soul has been waiting for.

Jack Ma's story isn't about luck; it's about perspective. What most people see as failure, innovators see as training. Problems are invitations in disguise. They carry the potential to call forth creativity, courage, and service that would otherwise remain hidden.

Think about it: every major breakthrough in history was born out of a problem.

- Diseases gave rise to medicine.
- Inequity gave rise to movements for justice.

- Isolation gave rise to technologies that connect us across continents.

Your greatest problems are not evidence that life is against you. They may be evidence that life is pointing you toward your purpose.

Mandela's Prison of Purpose

Few stories illustrate this truth more than Nelson Mandela's. For twenty-seven years he sat in a South African prison cell, condemned for daring to imagine freedom. Every day was a test of resolve. The walls could have crushed him, but instead they refined him. By the time he walked out of prison, he was not only a man seeking justice, but a man carrying vision. He refused bitterness and instead embraced reconciliation.

Mandela turned his greatest problem; the attempted silencing of his life, into an invitation to serve not only South Africa, but the world. His courage reminds us: sometimes the "prisons" in our lives are not punishments, but crucibles. They burn away what is inessential and forge us into leaders, healers, or innovators capable of transforming society.

What is your prison? Burnout? Debt? A pink slip you didn't expect. What if it is not an ending, but the very classroom preparing you for your next chapter?

Your Personal Thresholds

Perhaps your problem is not rejection letters or imprisonment. Perhaps your problem is subtler, quieter:

- A career that looks good on paper but feels hollow in your soul.
- A gnawing restlessness that no promotion, vacation, or bonus seems to cure.
- A daily life that drains more than it delights.

These are not inconveniences, they are signals. They are the soul's way of whispering: "You were made for more."

Burnout, in this light, is not failure. It is feedback. It is the body, mind, and spirit refusing to keep marching to a rhythm that doesn't belong to you.

Problems as Mirrors

Problems often mirror what we care about most. If you're constantly angered by inefficiency at work, maybe your gift is to bring order. If you're frustrated by shallow relationships, maybe your gift is to build community. If you're disillusioned by meaningless tasks, maybe your gift is to create enterprises where purpose thrives.

What you notice is not happenstance. It is patterned to your gifts. Jack Ma's gift of *optimism*, Fannie Lou Hamer's gift of *courage*, Maya Angelou's voice or the gift of *oration*, all were sharpened against the stone of problems. Without problems, gifts remain theoretical. With them, gifts become tangible, tested, and transformative.

The Archetypal Lens

I've based my work around the framework of Archetypes. Each of these Archetypes embodies ten "innate birth gifts". This concept will be elaborated on in the next chapter. I chose seven, as these correlate to specific laws and processes in nature. This will render 70 "innate birth gifts" to draw new inspiration and possibilities from. The seven archetypes offer a powerful way to see how problems invite gifts to be revealed:

- **Warrior** — Problems summon the gift of *courage*.
- **Sage** — Problems call for the gift of *wisdom*.
- **Seer** — Problems invite the gift of *vision*.
- **Scholar** — Problems require the gift of *introspection*.
- **King** — Problems demand leadership and the gift of *responsibility*.
- **Server** — Problems stir the gift of *compassion*.
- **Artisan** — Problems ignite the gift of *creativity*.

The problem you face may not be coincidental; it may be precisely what awakens your dominant archetypes and the corresponding innate birth gifts.

Reframing Failure

Failure is often disguised as the end-all to problems. But failure is rarely final, it's formative. Jack Ma's rejections refined his vision. Mandela's prison deepened his leadership.

Consider your own story. Which failures have shaped you most? Which disappointments have taught you truths no classroom could teach? Seen rightly, failure is a mentor. It strips us of illusions and forces us to ask deeper questions about who we are and what we're here for.

Reflection I

Take out a notebook and respond to these prompts:

1. List three problems that frustrate you most in your current work or life.

2. For each problem, ask: *What gift is this problem inviting me to use? (see table 6.1 in chapter 6 and "70 Gifts List" in appendix for full list)*

3. Reframe one past "failure" as a teacher. What did it show you about your resilience, creativity, or compassion?

These simple reflections can transform problems from weights into wings.

Reflection II

Where am I trying to pour new wine into old vessels in my own life?

Consider one area of your life where you feel tension or resistance. Ask yourself if you are trying to fit a new paradigm, new potential, or new purpose into an outdated form. What would it look like to create a new 'wineskin'; a new way of thinking, living, or leading—that could contain your greatness and significance?

Sacred Patrons and Problems

In the next chapter, we'll explore the idea of Sacred Patrons, the clients, communities, or causes you are most called to serve. Often, your Sacred Patrons are revealed through your problems. The frustrations you feel most intensely are often the very struggles they face. By solving your problem, you create solutions for theirs. By healing your wound, you offer medicine to the world.

Closing

Lincoln's reminder still stands: the assumptions of the past cannot carry the weight of the stormy present. Your problems are not signs of failure but signals of transformation—cracks in the old wineskin, evidence that you are meant to carry new wine. Just as Jack Ma turned rejection into innovation and Mandela turned imprisonment into vision, you too are invited to rise with the occasion. The difficulties in your life are not interruptions of your destiny; they are invitations into your greatness, your significance, and the new paradigms of purpose waiting to be born.

In the next chapter, we'll introduce the ideal of the innate birth gifts and archetypes that will help you rise to meet these invitations.

3

YOUR SECRET BIRTH GIFTS

""I counted everything. I counted the steps to the road, the steps up to church, the number of dishes and silverware I washed ... anything that could be counted, I did." — Katherine Johnson

Katherine Johnson was a quiet genius. Born in West Virginia in 1918, she loved counting from the moment she could walk. Numbers were her playground. She skipped grades, graduated high school at fourteen, and became one of the first Black women to work as a mathematician at NASA. There, she calculated flight trajectories that sent John Glenn into orbit and helped put the first men on the moon.

Johnson didn't seek fame. She simply followed her gift.

What looked ordinary to her, an ease with numbers; the gift of *arithmetic*, became extraordinary in the service of history. Her story reminds us that the gifts we carry, often unnoticed or undervalued, can shape destinies when they are brought to light.

You carry gifts like this too. They may not involve mathematics or space travel, but they are no less powerful. These gifts are not arbitrary skills. They are your birthright, woven into you before you even arrived. They are what I call your Secret Birth Gifts.

Remembering What You Already Knew

We don't need to create our gifts from scratch; we need to remember them. Children know this instinctively. Watch a child play, and you will see glimpses of their soul. They build, sing, teach, invent, nurture, or explore, not for reward, but for joy.

As adults, we forget. We trade imagination for responsibility, creativity for conformity, authenticity for approval. Yet those early sparks are never lost. They wait patiently for us to reclaim them.

Think back to your own childhood. What were you drawn to before the world told you who you "should" be?

For me, the signs were there early:

- **Daycare chalkboard**: I rushed to be the first to demonstrate my letters. I discovered the gift of *composition*, the power in expressing myself in writing.

- **Church recitations**: My chest swelled when my voice carried across the sanctuary each week after Sunday School. I was learning that words had power, not just to inform, but to inspire. I discovered the gift of *oration*.

- **Grandfather's farm**: Watching seeds transform into tomatoes, peppers, and watermelons taught me the mystery of nurture. Later, in my own backyard garden, I tasted the joy of cultivating life. I discovered the gift of *nature*.

- **Sketching cartoons**: Hours of drawing awakened my Artisan side. Ideas in my mind took form on paper. I discovered the gift of *art*.

At the time I saw these as just necessary assignments or hobbies. I would later come to understand that they were messages. Each pointed toward the gifts that would later fuel my purpose: composing, teaching, speaking, cultivating, creating, and later launching businesses.

How Gifts Speak

Your secret birth gifts often show up in three ways:

1. **Ease** — Activities you can do almost without trying.

2. **Joy** — Things that make you lose track of time.

3. **Impact** — Moments when others say, *"You're good at that."*

Katherine Johnson didn't struggle with math; it flowed. Fannie Lou Hamer didn't train to be fearless; courage burned in her bones. Maya Angelou didn't fabricate wisdom; silence carved it into her voice.

Your gifts speak in the same way. But the world often convinces us to ignore them, chasing instead what is "safe" or "practical." Burnout is often the result of betraying these gifts for too long.

Archetypes: The Language of Gifts

To make sense of how these gifts show up, I created the **Accessing Your Archetypes™ Assessment**. It centers around seven dominant archetypes:

- **Seer** — Vision, intuition, foresight.

- **Sage** — Wisdom, insight, perspective.

35

- **Warrior** — Courage, protection, perseverance.

- **Scholar** — Truth, clarity, knowledge.

- **King** — Leadership, authority, influence.

- **Server** — Compassion, service, healing.

- **Artisan** — Creativity, innovation, beauty.

These archetypes are not masks you put on, they are mirrors of who you already are. They help you see your gifts more clearly, and how they want to express themselves in the world. We won't go deep into the assessment here but understand this: your fire within (from Chapter 1) burns through these archetypes. They are the channels of your gifts, your natural strengths waiting to be awakened.

Rediscovering Your Own Gifts

I had to learn this the hard way. Like many professionals, I once silenced my birth gifts to climb the corporate ladder. The titles were impressive, the paycheck steady, but the fire dimmed. Only when I began reconnecting with those childhood sparks; teaching, speaking, cultivating, creating, did I begin to feel alive again.

The same is true for you. Rediscovery begins not with reinvention, but with remembrance.

Try this exercise:

1. Close your eyes and remember yourself at age 7 or 8. (or pick any age)

2. What activities made you smile widest?

3. What were you naturally drawn to when no one was telling you what to do?

4. What compliments or encouragement did you hear from teachers, parents, or friends?

Write them down. Even if they seem small, they are clues.

Gifts in Everyday Life

Birth gifts don't always shout. Sometimes they whisper. They show up when you're:

- The friend people call for advice (Sage).

- The one who notices solutions others overlook (Seer).

- The organizer everyone relies on (King).

- The caregiver who eases others' pain (Server).

- The creator who designs, builds, or beautifies (Artisan).

The secret isn't to force your gifts into someone else's mold, but to notice where they're already showing up.

Sacred Patrons and Your Gifts

Your gifts are not just for you; they are meant to serve others. The people who most need what you carry are your **Sacred Patrons**. They are drawn to your fire like travelers to a lighthouse.

The corporate world refers to these sacred patrons as customers, or clients. For me those titles are more transactional, sometimes without the true sense of caring for the outcome rather than the gain of profit from the transaction itself. Although I might use these words in practice, I think of them internally as sacred patrons.

Often, your sacred patrons are people who face the very struggles you've overcome. If your gift is *clarity*, they may be confused. If your gift is *courage*, they may be afraid. If your gift is *creation*, they may be stuck. Your gifts are answers to their problems.

When you honor your gifts, you do more than ignite your own fire, you light the way for those who are waiting for you.

Reflection: Reclaiming Your Gifts

Pause here and reflect:

- List three activities from childhood that made you feel alive.

- Identify one way you can practice each of these in your current life.

- Ask yourself: *Who might benefit if I offered this gift more fully?*

These are not abstract questions. They are invitations to reclaim what has always been yours.

Closing

Katherine Johnson changed history with her numbers. I began my own path with chalkboards, gardens, and cartoons. You have your own sparks; clues planted in childhood, waiting to be recognized as gifts.

Don't underestimate them. They may be the very tools you need to answer the problems you identified in the last chapter. They may be the bridge to your Sacred Patrons.

Your gifts are not an act of chance. They are your birthright. They are "the fire within" made visible. And once you reclaim them, you'll see that your purpose was never lost, it was always waiting inside you.

4

THE SWEET SPOT OF YOUR CALLING

When you engage in work that taps your talents and fuels your passion, that rises out of a great need in the world…therein lies your voice, your calling, your soul's code." — Stephen R. Covey

Viola Davis: Fire That Found Its Purpose

Viola Davis grew up in poverty in Rhode Island, often too hungry to focus in school, sometimes digging through trash bins for food. Yet she discovered her fire in acting. On stage, she could tell stories that mattered. Acting became more than a craft; it was her lifeline, her way of giving voice to people who rarely had one. She pursued her passion relentlessly, honing her skill until Hollywood could no longer ignore her.

But what makes Davis remarkable is not just her awards, it is how she wove passion with purpose. She used her platform to tell stories of resilience, injustice, and survival; stories that awaken empathy and courage in audiences worldwide. Passion by itself might have led her to fame. Passion joined with purpose made her a force for transformation.

This is the essence of calling: **when what you love intersects with what the world needs**.

Clarifying the Terms: Gifts vs. Talents

A common mistake is treating **gifts** and **talents** as the same thing. They are not.

- **Birth Gifts** are innate qualities that shape how you think, feel, and engage with the world. They require no training because they have always been part of you. Examples include deep empathy, a natural sense of justice, the ability to see patterns, or a magnetic leadership presence.

- **Talents** are learned and developed through practice. They are the skills you acquire, refine, and strengthen with effort. Examples include public speaking, coding, playing the violin, or mastering business strategy.

You are born with **gifts**, but you cultivate **talents**. Talents give your gifts tools of expression. Gifts are the wellspring, supply, or source; talents are the instruments, means or channel.

Confusing the two can be costly. If you try to build your life on talents alone, you may succeed for a while but end up restless, burnt out, or misaligned. When you root your work in your gifts and let talents serve them, you create something authentic and sustainable.

Passion and Purpose

Passion is personal. It's what excites you, energizes you, and makes you feel most alive. A hobby, an interest, or even a career might thrill you for a season, but passion by itself can fade if it lacks deeper meaning.

Purpose is larger. It is the contribution your passion makes when it is directed toward service. Purpose answers the question, *"Who benefits from my gifts and why does it matter?"*

- Passion without purpose burns out.

- Purpose without passion drains you.

- Passion joined with purpose creates calling.

The Four Elements of Calling

Your calling comes alive at the intersection of four elements:

1. **Gifts** — innate endowments you were born with.

2. **Talents** — skills you have cultivated and trained.

3. **Passion** — what excites you and fuels your energy.

4. **Purpose** — how your gifts, talents, and passion serve others.

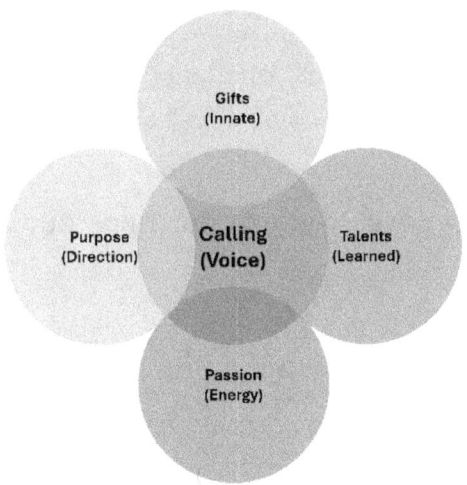

Figure 4.1: The Convergence of Calling

Your calling is discovered when gifts, talents, passion, and purpose converge.

- *Gifts provide the foundation.*

- *Talents provide the tools.*

- *Passion provides the energy.*

- *Purpose provides the direction.*
  Together, they form your **voice** — the unique expression of your life's work, the world most needs to hear.

The Archetypal Dimension

Each archetype expresses a natural alignment of passion and purpose:

- The **Warrior** loves challenge but finds purpose in protecting others.

- The **Sage** loves wisdom but finds purpose in guiding seekers.

- The **Seer** loves vision but finds purpose in pointing the way forward.

- The **Scholar** loves truth but finds purpose in uncovering clarity.

- The **King** loves leading but finds purpose in creating order for community.

- The **Server** loves helping but finds purpose in easing

suffering and restoring dignity to others.

- The **Artisan** loves creating but finds purpose in crafting beauty that uplifts.

Your archetypes reveal how your gifts and passions naturally align with service. They are clues to your *calling*.

Iyanla Vanzant: From Pain to Purpose

Iyanla Vanzant endured tremendous personal loss, including poverty and the death of her daughter. Out of that pain, she discovered her purpose: to help others heal. She could have stopped at passion — speaking, writing, teaching — but she aligned her passion with the greater purpose of restoring lives.

Her books, television work, and workshops became more than a career. They became a *calling*.

My Own Alignment

In my corporate years, I mistook success for calling. I worked hard, achieved titles, and earned the paycheck. But passion drained away because purpose was missing. I got trapped into what I see a lot of entrepreneurs doing—"chasing the bag", the hustle game!

When I began teaching, coaching, and writing, I rediscovered my fire. The joy I feel (passion) in this labor of love, is matched by the transformation I witness in others (purpose). This is when I understood: my calling is not just to succeed, but to help others find their own fire and build enterprises from it—and specifically; enterprises that serve humanity and make a lasting impact.

As I mentioned in the prologue, I was inspired by Stephen Covey's The 8th Habit, where he suggested that the next step to becoming effective was to find greatness. In this he suggested that the path to greatness was to find our "voice" and then help others find theirs. This became a mantra to me. I had indeed found my calling, and indeed the guiding motive for the next phase of my life!

Your story will look different, but the principle is the same. Where joy meets service, you find calling.

Service as the Heart of Calling

An African proverb says, *"If you want to go fast, go alone. If you want to go far, go together."*

Calling is never just about you. It's about the community your gifts serve. Viola Davis tells stories for people who were silenced. Iyanla Vanzant heals wounds for those who are hurting. Your Sacred Patrons — those you are uniquely called to serve — are waiting for you.

When passion burns only for self, it eventually burns out. When it burns for others, it becomes a steady flame.

Genuine Significant Value

Your **Genuine Significant Value** is the meeting place of three sacred currents: your core gifts, the pain or longing that stirs your compassion, and the transformation that naturally unfolds when you offer those gifts in service. It is the essence of what you give that truly matters.

Value is not what you think you offer; it is what others experience through you. It is the relief, the insight, or the renewal that flows from your authentic presence. Your skills and work are only the instruments; your Genuine Significant Value is the melody they play.

Ask yourself:

- Do I bring calm where there is confusion?

- Do I restore confidence where fear has taken root?

- Do I inspire courage where resignation has set in?

- Do I bring light where hope has dimmed?

When you see value through this lens, purpose takes on new form. It becomes love made visible. You recognize that your life's work is less about what you do and more about what happens in others because you showed up as your true self.

Reflection and Activation Exercise

Reflect on the following questions:

1. What gift do I naturally and consistently bring that offers comfort, strength, or clarity to others?

2. What transformation or renewal do people often experience when they encounter my authentic self?

3. How does this gift align with what the world seems to be asking of me now?

Now, write your **Genuine Significant Value Statement** using this framework:

"I help [describe the people or situations you feel called to serve] who are struggling with [specific pain or challenge] by offering [your natural gift or way of being], so they can experience [the transformation or inner state your presence evokes]."

Example:

"I help those who feel uncertain about their direction by offering gentle guidance and spiritual insight so they can rediscover clarity and trust their path."

Let this statement center you. It is the language of alignment. Knowing your Genuine Significant Value helps you discern where your passion and purpose meet—the sweet spot of your calling.

Exercises for Discernment

1. Write down three activities that bring you joy.

2. Write down three problems in the world that break your heart.

3. Look for overlap. Where do your joys meet the world's needs?

That overlap is the seed of calling.

Sacred Patrons and Calling

In Chapter 2, we introduced the concept of problems as invitations. In Chapter 3, we uncovered the gifts you already carry and introduced the next piece: your **Sacred Patrons**.

As a reminder, Sacred Patrons are those your calling is meant to serve. The corporate world refers to them as customers or clients. They are the people whose struggles match your gifts, whose struggles call forth your passion. Think of them as divine assignments — not just someone you're looking to engage in a monetary transaction that helps you to "secure the bag".

When your gifts and talents become a bridge between your joy and their need, you step fully into calling. It's not theory — it's a living relationship between who you are and who you're here for.

Closing

Viola Davis turned her passion for acting into a purpose of storytelling that gives voice to the voiceless. Iyanla Vanzant transformed her pain into a calling of healing. The same possibility lives in you.

Calling is not a mystery. It is the meeting point of what makes you come alive and what helps the world heal. Your "fire within" burns brightest at that intersection.

In the next chapter, we'll look at what happens when burnout enters the picture — and how to design a life without fear by aligning fully with your calling.

5

BEYOND BURNOUT:
DESIGNING A LIFE WITHOUT FEAR

"Whatever is bringing you down, get rid of it. Because you'll find that when you're free ... your true self comes out." — *Tina Turner*

Burnout is not the end. It is a beginning. It is your body, mind, and spirit conspiring to whisper, something must change.

We often treat burnout as shameful, as if exhaustion means weakness. In truth, burnout is a signal. It is not proof you have failed; it is proof you have given too much of yourself to something that no longer returns life in-kind. When burnout arrives, it is not an indictment. It is an invitation to redesign.

Tina Turner's Descent into Burnout

Few lives illustrate this truth better than Tina Turner's. She was a rising star in the 1960s and 70s, adored by audiences worldwide for her raw voice and stage presence. But behind the spotlight, her life was unraveling. Trapped in an abusive marriage with Ike Turner, she endured violence, manipulation, and exhaustion from grueling tours.

Tina later confessed she had nearly lost herself, her identity eroded by years of control and abuse. The fame was real, but so was the burnout. She reached a point where she no longer recognized the woman in the mirror.

Then came the turning point. She walked away with nothing but her name, leaving behind the money, fame, and the familiarity of a broken partnership. That decision could have destroyed her career. Instead, it saved her life.

Burnout as Redesign

Tina did not retreat from life. She redesigned it. She rebuilt her career from scratch, starting over in small venues while others whispered that her time had passed. In her forties, when most performers faded from view, she reinvented herself into a global icon, one of the most celebrated performers of all time.

The secret was not just her music, but her spirit. She turned to spiritual practices, chanting and meditation, to restore her inner strength. From that spiritual core, she rebuilt outward, free from fear and filled with resilience.

Burnout had not destroyed her. It had stripped away illusions and forced her into clarity. The Tina who emerged was not a victim, but a victor.

Redesign, Not Retreat

Tina's story shows us the truth: burnout does not require retreat, it requires redesign.

Retreat says, "I cannot keep going, so I will stop." Redesign says, "I cannot keep going this way, so I will create a new way."

That shift in perspective is life changing. Retreat empties you. Redesign empowers you.

Burnout as Preparation

In your own life, burnout can feel like a prison. But what if it is not punishment, but preparation? What if the fire you are walking through is shaping the leader, the innovator, the healer you are becoming? Burnout is an invitation—a call to redesign your life without fear.

Here, I introduce the **7-Step Awaken to Your Life Purpose Framework**, a guide to shift from fear and dependence on external "security" into freedom, clarity, and alignment. Like Tina Turner, who reimagined her entire life, and like Mandela, who saw beyond his cell walls, you too are invited to see beyond your current circumstances and imagine what could be.

This framework unfolds in **three phases** divided into seven steps. The first two phases are the most critical. Once these first two phases are clarified (see below), the third phase can be carried out with any of the most current business tools and logic.

Here is a simplified version of the seven-step framework. (another more detailed version is found in the appendix on page 122) You will also have the opportunity to reflect on and practice these steps in the **Reflection Exercise** at the end of this chapter. For those ready to take this further, an even deeper dive awaits in our coaching programs or through our self-paced online course found on our website: www.assurecoaching.online.

The 7-Step Awaken to Your Life Purpose Framework

Phase I – Find Your "Aha Moment"

1. **Identify Your Innate Gifts**
   Your gifts are your compass. The spark you were born with is still burning.

2. **Discover Your Passion**
   What stirs your soul? What excites you enough to lose track of time?

Phase II – Monetize Your Purpose

3. **Own Your Significance**
   Burnout erodes self-worth. This step rebuilds it. You matter, your gifts matter, your story matters.

4. **Monetize Your Passion**
   Purpose must sustain life. Translate gifts into streams of income that align with your values.

Phase III – Organize & Grow Your Enterprise –

this phase is only for the individual who aspires to launch an enterprise (for profit or non-profit). If this is not your desire, at this point in the process, you can identify an existing enterprise to align with to offer your passion and service.

5. **Organize Your Business**
   Build systems and structures that free you from chaos and give your vision stability.

6. **Systematize Your Process**
   Establish routines and models that allow you to grow without burning out again.

7. **Develop a Winning Team**
   No calling is fulfilled alone. Surround yourself with allies who believe in your mission and multiply your impact.

Tina walked a similar path. She rediscovered her gifts, reclaimed her passion, rebuilt her significance, and created a support system that carried her to new heights.

Turning Gifts into Business

For many professionals, fear of leaving a steady paycheck is paralyzing. Tina faced the same fear when she left Ike. She walked away with nothing. Yet she discovered that her gift — her voice, her artistry, her ability to move audiences — could sustain her.

I experienced a similar realization. For years, I treated my gifts for teaching, coaching, and writing as side interests. When I finally aligned them with business design, I found that what filled me with fire could also create prosperity. I doubled my income within months and was invited to travel to three countries outside the U.S. within the next six months for pleasure and business opportunities.

Your gifts are not meant to be hobbies. They are meant to become enterprises of service. When aligned with your Sacred Patrons, they sustain both you and the people who need you most.

Your Social Value Proposition

Your **Social Value Proposition (SVP)** is the heartbeat of

your service to the world. It blends your Genuine Significant Value with your larger mission—capturing not only what you do and who you serve, but the change you are committed to creating.

This is the moment when your purpose takes form in the world. It is no longer just an inner fire; it becomes a light that guides others. Your SVP reminds you that your gifts are not yours to keep—they are meant to ripple outward into healing, growth, and transformation.

Use this framework to craft your own Social Value Proposition Statement:

"I exist to [describe your deeper contribution or service] by using my gift of [name your gift or capacity] to serve [Sacred Patron audience] who are seeking relief from [pain or problem], so they may experience [transformation or gain] and contribute to a more [values-aligned outcome for society]."

Example:

"I exist to inspire healing and empowerment by using my gift of Compassion to serve women navigating burnout and self-doubt, so they may experience inner peace, renewed energy, and contribute to a more balanced and heart-centered culture."

This statement is more than a declaration—it is your

compass. As you design or align your life's work, it ensures that every decision and partnership reflects your purpose and your Sacred Patrons' highest good.

Sacred Patrons

Tina's patrons were not abstract. They were her audiences, especially women who drew courage from her resilience. She did not just sing, she inspired. Her Sacred Patrons were those who saw in her survival, the hope of their own.

Your Sacred Patrons are waiting too. They are the people whose struggles match your gifts. They are not just clients; they are divine assignments. When you serve them, you fulfill purpose, not just career.

Touch a Million…Make a Million

There is a simple but profound equation I call the **Equation of Enrichment**: *to the degree that you enrich the lives of others, you will in turn be enriched.* Think of yourself as a walking, living, breathing enterprise — a "million-dollar enterprise" by design.

The principle is straightforward. If you touch the lives of one million people and they in turn enrich you with one dollar each, you will have earned one million dollars. Or perhaps you serve one hundred thousand people with a $10 product, ten thousand people with a $100 service, or even one thousand clients with a $1,000 offer. **See Table 5.1**. However you frame it, the equation works.

The point is not about the numbers, but about the **value exchange**. When you decide how your gifts can be transformed into talents, and how those talents can be channeled into a service or product that genuinely enriches others, you have unlocked the path to sustainable success. By the **Law of Compensation**, what you give inevitably returns — often multiplied.

So, the real question becomes: what gift will you develop into a talent, what product or service will you offer, and how will you begin enriching lives? When you commit to that journey, you will not only build an enterprise of value, you will also discover that touching lives at scale is the surest way to touch your own abundance.

Reflection: The Equation of Enrichment

If you were to enrich the lives of 10,000 people with your gift, what service or product would you offer them? How would you ensure that what you create genuinely improves their lives? Take a few moments to sketch out ideas. Remember, the number isn't the point — the principle is.

With every life you enrich, you move closer to building your "million-dollar enterprise" — and to embodying the purpose you were born to fulfill.

Table 5.1: Touch a Million...Make a Million

Price of Service/Product	Number of Lives Enriched	Gross Value (USD)
$1	1,000,000	$1,000,000
$10	100,000	$1,000,000
$100	10,000	$1,000,000
$1,000	1,000	$1,000,000

Letting Go of Mistakes

Tina once admitted she stayed too long in a destructive partnership. For years, she blamed herself. But in time, she realized those mistakes did not define her. They refined her.

Mistakes are not chains. They are teachers. As an African proverb says, *"Do not look where you fell, look where you slipped."* Failure is not final. It is formative. It shows you where to adjust the path, not abandon it.

When you let go of mistakes, you release fear. You no longer need perfection to move forward. Progress becomes enough.

Burnout as Rebirth

Think of burnout as fire clearing a forest. It feels destructive, but it makes way for new growth. The soil of your soul becomes fertile again.

Tina Turner's rebirth is proof. Out of the ashes of burnout, she planted seeds of clarity, courage, and calling. The woman who once felt trapped became the woman who sang, *"What's Love Got to Do with It,"* and electrified the world.

Burnout is not the death of purpose. It is the birthplace of a fearless new chapter.

Reflection Exercise

Identify one area of life that feels burned out.

Ask yourself: is this a retreat moment or a redesign moment?

Choose one of the seven steps and begin practicing it this week. (For assistance in identifying your gifts, see chapter 6)

Like Tina, small steps can lead to transformation that the world once thought impossible.

Closing

Tina Turner's life was proof that burnout is not the end. She walked through exhaustion, abuse, and fear, and emerged stronger, freer, and more radiant than ever.

Her story is your reminder. Burnout is a signal to let go of what no longer serves you and to redesign life around your gifts, your passions, and your Sacred Patrons and the product and/or service you will create to serve them.

Beyond burnout lies freedom. Beyond fear lies faith. Beyond exhaustion lies empowerment.

Your fire within is not waiting to be extinguished. It is waiting to be reborn.

6

THE FIRST STEP IS CLARITY

*"I don't want to be thought of as the 'girl who was shot by the Taliban';
I want to be the girl who fought for the rights of every child, whether girl
or boy, the right of education and the right of equality."* — Malala
Yousafzai

Malala Yousafzai was just fifteen when a bullet tried to
silence her vision. She had spoken out for the right of girls in
Pakistan to receive education, and extremists responded with
violence. But instead of shrinking back, she rose higher. Her
clarity of vision — education for every child — gave her a
courage that defied death itself. Today, her name is
synonymous with hope and possibility.

The attempt on her life sparked an international outpouring
of support. After being stabilized in Pakistan, she was flown

nearly 3,600 miles to a hospital in Birmingham, UK, where she continued her recovery. Global media declared her "the most famous teenager in the world." Fifty leading Muslim clerics in Pakistan issued a legal ruling condemning the attack, while governments, human rights organizations, and feminist groups worldwide denounced the Taliban. In defiance, the Taliban vowed a second assassination attempt — an act that only intensified international outrage.

Yet Malala did not retreat into fear. Instead, she stepped more boldly into her calling. From her new home in Birmingham, she co-founded the Malala Fund, co-authored the best-selling memoir *I Am Malala*, and received honors including the Sakharov Prize, honorary Canadian citizenship, and, most notably, the Nobel Peace Prize — making her, at seventeen, the youngest-ever laureate. Her story shows us that clarity always comes before courage. Without it, we drift, hesitate, or hide. With it, we act. Malala's life reminds us that clarity of purpose, even when opposed, unleashes a power that nothing can suppress.

Reflection: What truth in your own life is so clear, so undeniable, that even fear could not make you turn away from it?

Why Clarity Matters

Burnout clouds the mind. Passion without direction leads to frustration. Purpose without clarity becomes vague. But clarity cuts through the fog. It does three things:

1. **Focuses Energy** — You stop scattering effort and start channeling it.
2. **Reveals Priorities** — You know what to say yes to and what to decline.
3. **Creates Courage** — When you see the path clearly, fear loses its grip.

Without clarity, even the brightest gifts remain hidden. With clarity, even the simplest step becomes powerful.

Clarity and the Archetypes

This is where the **Accessing Your Archetypes™ Assessment** comes in. It is designed to help you gain clarity about who you are at your core.

Your archetypes reveal:

1. **How you act** – Active Archetype
2. **Where you draw knowledge** – Passive Archetype
3. **What motivates you** – Mediating Archetype

These are explained in more detail in the assessment report

you will receive once you complete the online digital assessment. There is also a companion e-book, "7 Archetypes for Unlocking Your Life Purpose" that goes into even greater detail offered with the assessment or purchased separately from our website.

When these three align — how you act, what you know, and what motivates you — clarity is born. You see yourself without distortion. You know your gifts, your patterns, and your potential.

Clarity Through Your Innate Gifts

So, let's discuss the assessment tool for you to discover how to bring clarity to your own gifts and destiny. Through the **Accessing Your Archetypes™ Assessment**, you will identify your three dominant archetypes, your compass for who you are beyond the corporate world, what motivates you, and where you draw knowledge. With clarity, you will know how to activate your inner gifts, the fire within.

Listed in **Table 6.1** are the innate gifts associated with each of the seven primary archetypes. Each archetype embodies 10 specific gifts, totaling 70 innate gifts across all archetypes. These gifts are the core of the assessment and serve as a crucial tool in helping you better understand yourself, your strengths, your preferences, and how you naturally show up in the world. This is the beginning step in truly discovering the fire within. It is with this tool, this instrument, that you will gain deeper clarity and understanding of who you are beyond Corporate America.

Table 6.1: The Seven Archetypes and Their Innate Gifts

Seer
- Circumspection
- Discernment
- Enterprise
- Intuition
- Justice
- Mysticism
- Optimism
- Organization
- Reassurance
- Vision

Sage
- Counsel
- Generosity
- Gentility
- Integrity
- Nurture
- Patience
- Prudence
- Serenity
- Temperance
- Wisdom

Warrior
- Athleticism
- Constancy
- Courage
- Devotion
- Discipline
- Focus
- Fortitude
- Protectorship
- Resolve
- Vigilance

Scholar
- Credibility
- Gnosis
- Inquiry
- Introspection
- Nature
- Observation
- Oration
- Reform
- Rhetoric
- Sensibility

King
- Efficiency
- Excellence
- Humanity
- Influence
- Nobility
- Pacification
- Responsibility
- Shrewdness
- Solace
- Stability

Server
- Altruism
- Benevolence
- Compassion
- Cordiality
- Dedication
- Diplomacy
- Empathy
- Enthusiasm
- Healing
- Supportiveness

Artisan
- Aesthetics
- Arithmetic
- Art
- Cheer
- Composition
- Creation
- Geometry
- Industry
- Music
- Precision

By engaging with both this list and the detailed profiles of the innate gifts in the appendix, you will be empowered to embrace your archetypal identity and use this knowledge to navigate your purpose with enhanced self-awareness and confidence.

Each person's combined gift set is distinct, shaped by their experiences, passions, and talents. By becoming more aware of these inherent strengths, we can learn to harness them more intentionally, making a lasting impact in both small, daily interactions and larger, life-altering endeavors.

Reflection: Once you have taken the assessment, come back and ask yourself, *what truth in your life is so clear, so undeniable, that even fear could not make you turn away from it?*

My Search for Clarity

For years, I sought clarity in external places: job titles, salaries, promotions, career changes and more. They gave me temporary direction, but not fulfillment. Only when I began reconnecting with my innate gifts and mapping them through the archetypes did I discover true clarity.

I realized my gifts were among others, the gifts of inquiry, humanity, and enterprise. My dominant archetypes: Scholar, King, and Seer, gave me language for what I already sensed.

That clarity gave me confidence. Confidence gave me courage. Courage gave me a new path. That new path for me is one of Coaching others to find their voice! Nothing in the world is more important than this at this point in my life. I truly gained the clarity to discern my life purpose beyond Corporate America!

The same will happen for you.

Malala's Lesson

Malala did not wait for perfect conditions. She had clarity of purpose, that education is a right. That clarity gave her courage to act, even when the cost was great.

Your clarity may not put you on a global stage, and hopefully it will not bring violence into your life, but it **will** give you the courage to step into the life you are called to live. It may give you the boldness to leave a job that drains you, to launch a business that excites you, or to serve patrons who need your fire.

The Spiral of Clarity, Confidence, Courage

- Clarity is not the end. It is the beginning of a spiral that grows stronger:
- **Clarity** gives you **confidence**

- Confidence fuels **courage**
- Courage leads to **action**
- Action creates more **clarity**

The more you act in alignment with your gifts, the clearer you become.

Reflection: Finding Your Clarity

Take some time with these questions:

1. What gifts have shown up consistently in your life?
2. Which archetypes describe how you act, think, and are motivated.
3. If fear were not in the way, what would clarity tell you to do next?

Write your answers. Then read them aloud. Hearing your own voice speak your truth makes clarity real.

Closing Summary

By embracing and intentionally expressing your unique gifts in every aspect of life, you contribute to a more harmonious, compassionate, and vibrant world. Each gift offers an avenue for growth, connection, and service, reminding us that gifts and talents are not just for personal fulfillment but for enhancing the lives of others.

As you apply these insights, consider how your gifts can be woven into the fabric of your daily life, transforming routine moments into opportunities for creativity, kindness, and impact. The true value of your gifts lies not just in possessing them, but in how you choose to share them with the world.

When you recognize your abilities as tools for positive change, you unlock new possibilities for yourself and for those around you. This chapter has served as both a guide and an invitation to step fully into your gifts, embracing the unique contributions you are equipped to make in your relationships, your work, and the world at large.

To begin this journey of clarity, visit
henryshelton.com/product/accessing-your-archetypes-assessment and take the *Accessing Your Archetypes*™ *Assessment*.
This tool will help you identify your dominant archetypes and
provide personalized insights into your strengths,
motivations, and the pathways toward a fulfilling, purpose-driven life.

After completing the assessment, you will gain clarity,
confidence, and courage to pursue your endeavors. For
further insight, (**ONLY AFTER TAKING THE ASSESSMENT**)
consider scheduling a one-on-one consultation at
henryshelton.com/consultation, where you will receive
personal guidance in applying this knowledge to your unique
circumstances and aspirations.

Take the first step today and unlock the path to living your
true purpose with clarity, confidence, and courage.

7

YOU ALREADY HOLD THE KEY

In the course of history, there comes a time when humanity is called to shift to a new level of consciousness…a time when we have to shed our fear and give hope to each other…that time is now" — *Wangari Maathai*

Wangari Maathai was born in a rural Kenyan village where opportunities for women were nearly nonexistent. In her community, girls were expected to marry young, work the land, and remain in the shadows. By every measure, her path was supposed to be limited, her voice unheard.

But Wangari carried a key that no circumstance could take from her. With determination, she pursued education, first in her village school, then through scholarships that led her all the way to the United States. When she returned to Kenya, she became the first woman in East and Central Africa to earn a PhD. Her achievements broke barriers, but they also drew criticism and resistance.

She faced setbacks that would have silenced most: government harassment, imprisonment for her activism, dismissal as "just a woman." Each obstacle could have locked the door to her destiny. Yet every time, Wangari turned the key within herself — courage, vision, resilience — and an unshakable belief in the power of ordinary people.

From those humble beginnings, she founded the **Green Belt Movement**, which went on to plant more than fifty million trees, empower women, and transform communities across Africa. Her efforts not only restored ecosystems but also restored dignity to countless lives. In 2004, Wangari Maathai was awarded the **Nobel Peace Prize**, becoming the first African woman to receive the honor, global recognition of a life lived with courage and purpose.

Her story reminds us that the key to transformation is not found in privilege, permission, or perfect conditions. It is carried inside, waiting to be turned through courage and action.

What is the Key?

The key is not another certification, another degree, or another corporate title. The key is clarity about your gifts and the courage to use them.

Maathai's simple vision of planting trees showed that world-changing action often begins with a single, ordinary act. Each tree was both a seed of change and a symbol of resilience.

The key is within you. It is your fire, your gifts, your archetypes, your patrons, your story.

Why We Miss It

Many of us believe the key is outside:

- in someone else's approval,

- in a perfect plan,

- in waiting for the "right" time.

But waiting is a form of fear. The truth is that you already have what you need to begin.

Your Warrior has **courage**.
Your Sage has **wisdom.**
Your Seer has **vision**.
Your Scholar has **clarity**.
Your King has **leadership**.

Your Server has **compassion**.

Your Artisan has **creativity**.

The door is waiting. (It could be your next opportunity, your next path, or your "Second Act" in your career) The key is in your hand.

The Three-Dominant Archetype Model

This is why the **three-dominant archetype model** is so important. Each of us has three archetypes that work together as a compass:

- One governs how we act (Active).

- One governs what we know (Passive).

- One governs what motivates us (Mediating).

When you understand your three-dominant pattern, you realize the key is not generic, it is uniquely yours. It tells you how to move, what knowledge to draw on, and what motivation fuels you. This combination unlocks your calling in ways no external system can dictate. It literally makes you one of **ten million** possible profile combinations!

Everyday Keys

Maathai's key was service through trees. Yours might be:

- The Scholar's gift of truth, clarifying what is confused.

- The Server's compassion, healing what is broken.

- The Artisan's creativity, imagining what does not yet exist.

The form may be different, but the principle is the same: when you use your key, doors open.

Reflection: Finding Your Key

Take time with these prompts:

1. What do people consistently thank you for?

2. What do you do that feels so natural, you hardly notice it?

3. What gift of yours, if withheld, would leave the world poorer?

The answers point to your key.

You Already Hold It

Wangari Maathai did not wait for permission. She trusted what she carried and acted. When the government tried to silence her, she planted more trees. When she was imprisoned, she emerged even more determined. When her critics dismissed her as "just a woman," she responded with action that reshaped a nation and inspired the world.

The same is true for you. You do not need to wait until everything is clear. You already hold the key. The fire within you is enough. The archetypes within you are enough. Your patrons are waiting.

The invitation is simple: use the key.

Closing

By now you have discovered the fire within, recognized problems as invitations, remembered your secret gifts, aligned passion with purpose, redesigned life beyond burnout, and clarified your path through your archetypes.

The journey has brought you here, to this truth: **you already hold the key**.

When you use it, you do more than unlock your own purpose. You light the way for others. You become part of a collective turning, sparks igniting into a blaze of transformation.

Your destiny is not locked away. It is waiting for you to use what you already carry.

You hold the key. Now is the time to turn it. And remember: every seed of courage you plant grows into a forest of transformation.

CONCLUSION
THE FIRE IS YOURS

You began this journey by encountering "the fire within", the quiet, powerful energy that has been with you since childhood. Perhaps at first it felt distant, buried under years of routine, responsibilities, or the weight of expectations. But as you've turned these pages, that fire has flickered back into view.

You have seen how problems are not punishments but invitations, how rejection, burnout, or disappointment can point the way to your calling. You have remembered your secret birth gifts, the sparks planted in you long before anyone told you who you should be. You have recognized how passion and purpose meet to create calling, and how burnout can become a gateway to redesign, not retreat. You have gained clarity, through your archetypes, about the gifts you carry and how they shape your destiny. You've learned how you are one in ten million! And you have discovered that the key to your future is not outside of you, it is already in your hands.

A Journey of Awakening

This has not been a book of theories. It has been a map, a way of awakening to what you already hold.

- **Chapter 1** reminded you that the fire within is real, alive, and waiting.

- **Chapter 2** reframed problems as invitations, thresholds that guide you.

- **Chapter 3** brought you back to childhood gifts and introduced the power of your secret inner birth gifts

- **Chapter 4** revealed that your calling lies at the intersection of passion, purpose, gifts, and talent.

- **Chapter 5** showed how burnout can lead to redesign, not retreat.

- **Chapter 6** gave you clarity through your archetypes and innate gifts.

- **Chapter 7** affirmed that you already hold the key.

Each chapter has been part of a larger spiral; clarity, confidence, courage, and calling.

The Invitation

Now the invitation is yours to accept. What will you do with this fire?

Will you ignore it, tucking it away until burnout forces change again? Or will you tend it, feed it, and let it guide your next chapter?

The fire within is not meant only for you. It is meant to light the way for others, your Sacred Patrons, your family, your community, your world. When you share your gifts, when you align your fire with service, you create ripples that extend far beyond your own life.

A Collective Movement

Wangari Maathai planted trees one by one, and they became a forest. Nelson Mandela endured prison walls, and his vision opened a nation to freedom. Tina Turner broke free from abuse and burnout, and her voice shook the world with resilience and joy. Fannie Lou Hamer declared she was "sick and tired of being sick and tired," and her cry became a rallying force in the Civil Rights Movement. Katherine

Johnson counted numbers as a girl, and her calculations carried astronauts to the stars. Malala Yousafzai refused silence, and her courage sparked movements for education worldwide.

Each began small. Each trusted the fire within. Each used the key they already carried.

You are invited into this same potpourri of stories.

A Call to Action

Here are your next steps:

1. **Reflect** — Revisit your gifts, your archetypes, your patrons. Journal, meditate, or pray about how they are showing up today.

2. **Act** — Choose one small action this week that aligns with your gifts. Send a message, start a draft, make an introduction.

3. **Serve** — Ask yourself, *WHO am I called to serve right now?* Then offer your gift to them. No need to wait for launching an enterprise, just serve!

4. **Grow** — Consider deepening your journey through the *Accessing Your Archetypes™ Assessment* and coaching opportunities designed to help you translate gifts into enterprises.

The journey does not end with this book. It begins here.

Closing Words

The fire within you is not fragile. It has survived disappointment, fear, disillusionment, and silence. It is still burning, ready to guide you into a life of clarity, confidence, courage, and calling.

Your gifts are not accidents. Your archetypes are not labels. They are compasses, pointing you toward the people you are called to serve and the difference you are destined to make.

You already hold the key. Use it. Unlock the doors waiting before you. Step into the life that has been waiting for you all along.

The fire within is yours.

Tend it. Share it.

Let it light the world.

APPENDICES

(Reference Tools)

- 70 Gifts List
- 7 Primary Archetypes Guide
- 7-Step Framework Diagram
- Human Needs Levels
- Industry Sectors Analysis

70 Gifts List

Details of the Inner Innate Birth Gifts of the **SEER**

CIRCUMSPECTION

The gift of Circumspection characterizes a person who is watchful and discreet; cautious; prudent and having well considered a thing.

DISCERNMENT

The gift of Discernment characterizes a person that demonstrates outstanding judgment and understanding; and can distinguish by sight, intellect, or some other sense.

ENTERPRISE

The gift of Enterprise characterizes a person with great imagination or initiative; someone who is ready to undertake projects of importance or difficulty or untried schemes, and energetic in carrying out any undertaking.

INTUITION

The gift of Intuition characterizes a person exhibiting the ability to have a direct perception of truth, fact, etc., independent of any reasoning process or objective, obvious, observable, or demonstrable proof or evidence.

JUSTICE

The gift of Justice characterizes a person guided by truth, reason, justice, and fairness.

MYSTICISM

The gift of Mysticism characterizes a person having the ability to discern the nature of reality, God, truth, etc. by direct revelation, intuition, or spiritual insight, without the medium of the senses or reason.

OPTIMISM

The gift of Optimism characterizes a person disposed to take a favorable view of events or conditions and to expect the most favorable outcome despite obvious or perceived problems or challenges.

ORGANIZATION

The gift of Organization characterizes a person who forms into a whole from interdependent or coordinated parts, persons, units, groups, or components, especially for united action or creation.

REASSURANCE

The gift of Reassurance characterizes a person who can inspire with confidence and spirit; one who can stimulate by assistance and approval; and can promote, advance, or foster confidence in a person.

VISION

The gift of Vision characterizes a person who has the ability to anticipate that which will or may come to be and being able to see a thing, event, or otherwise future developments long before they are obvious to most.

Details of the Inner Innate Birth Gifts of the **SAGE**

COUNSEL

The gift of Counsel characterizes a person skilled at giving advice; opinion or instruction in directing the judgment or conduct of another.

GENEROSITY

The gift of Generosity characterizes a person who is liberal in giving or sharing; unselfish; and free from meanness or smallness of mind or character.

GENTILITY

The gift of Gentility characterizes a person who is kind, has or shows pleasant, good-natured personal qualities; is friendly, and sociable.

INTEGRITY

The gift of Integrity characterizes a person adhering to rectitude; righteous, honest, or just; being in accord with what is right: always behaving honestly and having high moral standards.

NURTURE

The gift of Nurture characterizes a person inclined towards the process of caring for and encouraging the growth or development of someone or something.

PATIENCE

The gift of Patience characterizes a person who can endure or bear provocation, annoyance, misfortune, delay, hardship, pain, etc. with fortitude and calm and without complaint, anger, or the like.

PRUDENCE

The gift of Prudence characterizes a person who is wise or judicious in practical affairs; careful in providing for the future; discreet or circumspect; provident; sagacious; and sober.

SERENITY

The gift of Serenity characterizes a person who embodies the state of being calm, peaceful, tranquil; and unruffled.

TEMPERANCE

The gift of Temperance describes a person who is characterized by moderation as regards behavior, opinion, statement, indulgence of appetite, or passion.

WISDOM

The gift of Wisdom characterizes a person who has the quality of making sound decisions and taking intelligent action employing the application of experience, knowledge, and good judgment.

Details of the Inner Innate Birth Gifts of the WARRIOR

ATHLETICISM

The gift of Athleticism characterizes a person who is physically active and strong; capable of using physical skills, strength, agility, and stamina.

CONSTANCY

The gift of Constancy characterizes a person who is faithful to one's oath, commitments, vows, allegiance, or obligations.

COURAGE

The gift of Courage is characterized by the quality of mind or spirit that enables a person to face difficulty, danger, pain, etc., without fear; or bravery.

DEVOTION

The gift of Devotion characterizes a person who is zealous or ardent in attachment, loyalty, or affection.

DISCIPLINE

The gift of Discipline characterizes a person having or exhibiting the ability to act following steady, focused rigor, rules, etc. under a myriad of circumstances and showing a controlled form of behavior or way of working.

FOCUS

The gift of Focus characterizes a person showing great care and perseverance; constant in application or effort; working diligently at a task; persevering; industrious; and attentive.

FORTITUDE

The gift of Fortitude characterizes the strength of mind that enables a person to encounter danger, bear pain, and adversity, and courageously remain steadfast and unwavering.

PROTECTORSHIP

The gift of Protectorship characterizes a person who defends or acts as a guardian for another or one's property.

RESOLVE

The gift of Resolve describes a person who is characterized by firmness and determination in purpose or intent.

VIGILANCE

The gift of Vigilance characterizes a person who has the quality of being keenly watchful and alert, especially in avoiding danger.

Details of the Inner Innate Birth Gifts of the SCHOLAR

CREDIBILITY

The gift of Credibility characterizes a person who has the quality of being trusted and believed in.

GNOSIS

The gift of Gnosis characterizes a person who has much knowledge; scholarly, well-informed, connected or involved with the pursuit of knowledge.

INQUIRY

The gift of Inquiry is characterized by the quality of having the ability and love to search for information, facts, and principles through research.

INTROSPECTION

The gift of Introspection is characterized by the ability to engage in extended, contemplative reflection on one's thoughts and feelings.

NATURE

The gift of Nature characterizes a person with a love for and keen knowledge of the natural world with little or no formal schooling on the matter.

OBSERVATION

The gift of Observation characterizes a person prone to noticing or perceiving persons, situations, or otherwise carefully to gain information.

ORATION

The gift of Oration depicts a person skilled at giving formal public speeches, characterized by a studied or elevated style, diction, or delivery.

REFORM

The gift of Reform characterizes a person devoted to bringing about the improvement or amendment of what is wrong, corrupt, unsatisfactory, etc.

RHETORIC

The gift of Rhetoric describes a person endowed with the art or skill of speaking or writing formally and effectively, especially as a way to persuade or influence people.

SENSIBILITY

The gift of Sensibility characterizes a person having an acute perception of or responsiveness toward something, such as the emotions of another.

.Details of the Inner Innate Birth Gifts of the **KING**

EFFICIENCY

The gift of Efficiency characterizes a person performing or functioning in the best possible manner with the least waste of time and effort while using requisite knowledge, skill, and industry.

EXCELLENCE

The gift of Excellence characterizes a person committed to the highest degree of proficiency, skill, or excellence (moral, religious, political) or otherwise.

HUMANITY

The gift of Humanity is characterized by a person having a strong interest in or concern for human welfare, values, and dignity.

INFLUENCE

The gift of Influence is characterized by a person having the capacity to affect the character, development, or behavior of someone or something.

NOBILITY

The gift of Nobility characterizes a person having or showing fine personal qualities or high moral principles and ideals.

PACIFICATION

The gift of Pacification characterizes a person proficient at establishing or reestablishing peace, tranquility, quiet, or calm within a governed population divided or impacted by military, political, economic, or social disorder.

RESPONSIBILITY

The gift of Responsibility characterizes a person who understands the duty of taking measures with due foresight to plan for providing means of support, money, or otherwise to someone or something.

SHREWDNESS

The gift of Shrewdness characterizes a person who is astute and demonstrates keen, sharp, and clever powers of judgment in practical matters.

SOLACE

The gift of Solace describes a person who helps to soothe, console, reassure, and bring cheer to others.

STABILITY

The gift of Stability characterizes a person in a good state or condition that is not easily changed or likely to change, nor subject to material or emotional instabilities.

Details of the Inner Innate Birth Gifts of the **SERVER**

ALTRUISM

The gift of Altruism characterizes a person with the belief in or practice of disinterested and selfless concern for the well-being of others.

BENEVOLENCE

The gift of Benevolence characterizes a person committed to expressing goodwill, kindness, and charity as a means of helping others.

COMPASSION

The gift of Compassion is characterized by a person having or showing a feeling of deep sympathy and sorrow for another who is stricken by misfortune, accompanied by a strong desire to alleviate the suffering.

CORDIALITY

The gift of Cordiality is characterized by a person having or showing a pleasant, warm, kind, and friendly disposition.

DEDICATION

The gift of Dedication characterizes a person having or showing strong, earnest support for or loyalty to someone or something.

DIPLOMACY

The gift of Diplomacy characterizes a person skilled at dealing with sensitive matters or people tactfully without offending, upsetting, or arousing hostility.

EMPATHY

The gift of Empathy characterizes a person with the ability to create an emotional connection by recognizing, understanding, and sharing the thoughts and feelings of others.

ENTHUSIASM

The gift of Enthusiasm characterizes a person cheerfully consenting and displaying an energetic interest in a particular subject or activity and a desire to be involved in it.

HEALING

The gift of Healing describes a person who has a passion for the process of making others whole, healthy, sound, and free from injury or disease.

SUPPORTIVENESS

The gift of Supportiveness characterizes a person fond of giving or rendering aid, assistance, or service and making it easier for others to do their job or deal with a challenge or problem.

Details of the Inner Innate Birth Gifts of the ARTISAN

AESTHETICS

The gift of Aesthetics is characterized by a person having a love of beauty, and taste, and is responsive to or appreciative of what is pleasurable to the senses.

ARITHMETIC

The gift of Arithmetic characterizes a person who is an expert in the properties, method, or process of computation and manipulation of numbers in counting and calculation.

ART

The gift of Art is characterized by a person having a proclivity for the various branches of creative expression of the visual arts, literary arts, and performing arts.

CHEER

The gift of Cheer is characterized by a person having good spirits; pleasant, bright, hearty, ungrudging; having or showing a good mood or disposition; a person who is always fun to work with and a pleasure to be around.

COMPOSITION

The gift of Composition characterizes a person who has the skill of combining distinct parts or elements to form a whole.

CREATION

The gift of Creation characterizes a person who evolves results from one's thought or imagination and causes to come into being, meaningful new ideas, forms, methods, and interpretations.

GEOMETRY

The gift of Geometry characterizes a person skilled at the branch of mathematics that deals with the measurement, properties, and relationships of points, lines, angles, surfaces, solids, and higher dimensional analogs.

INDUSTRY

The gift of Industry characterizes a person who works earnestly, energetically, devotedly, and diligently and produces productive outcomes.

MUSIC

The gift of Music describes a person who demonstrates a mastery in the science or art of ordering vocal or instrumental sounds or both to produce a composition having beauty of form, and expression of emotion through the elements of rhythm, melody, and harmony.

PRECISION

The gift of Precision characterizes a person who has the quality of taking or showing extreme care about minute details in their ways and means of doing things.

7 PRIMARY ARCHETYPES GUIDE

This chapter delves into the seven primary archetypes, offering an in-depth exploration of their defining attributes and key characteristics. Each archetype has a unique essence, and by understanding the qualities associated with the one you resonate with, you will gain greater clarity on how to align with your true archetypal nature.

In the first section, I will present a detailed profile of each archetype. These profiles include their distinctive traits and attributes, which are essential in understanding and embodying the essence of the archetype you have assessed as being most aligned with. This will provide you with valuable insights to deepen your connection to your archetype and further clarify your alignment with it.

Following this, the second section will outline the innate gifts associated with each of the seven primary archetypes. Each archetype embodies 10 specific gifts, totaling 70 innate gifts across all archetypes. These gifts are the core of the assessment and serve as a crucial tool in helping you better understand yourself—your strengths, your preferences, and how you naturally show up in the world.

By engaging with both the detailed profiles and the innate gifts, you will be empowered to embrace your archetypal identity and use this knowledge to navigate your purpose with enhanced self-awareness and confidence.

Author's Fair Use Acknowledgment: Short excerpts in the sections titled *"Corresponding Cosmic Processes"* are drawn from Rodney Collin's *The Theory of Celestial Influence* (1954), Vincent Stuart Ltd. and Mercury Publications, Inc. They are used in a transformative manner to connect Collin's description of cosmic processes with the archetypal principles explored throughout this work.

If you haven't already done so, and would like to begin the journey of discovering your own unique archetype profile to activate your life's purpose, visit our website (https://henryshelton.com/product/accessing-your-archetypes-assessment/) and take the "Accessing Your Archetypes" assessment. This assessment is designed to help you identify your dominant archetypes and provide personalized insights into your strengths, motivations, and how they can guide you toward a more fulfilling and purpose-driven life. After completing the assessment, you'll gain clarity, confidence, and courage to pursue your endeavors. For further insight, (**ONLY AFTER TAKING THE ASSESSMENT**) consider scheduling a one-on-one consultation at henryshelton.com/consultation, where you will receive personal guidance in applying this knowledge to your unique circumstances and aspirations.

Take the first step today and unlock the path to living your true purpose with clarity, confidence, and courage.

SEER

The Seer archetype is often associated with intuition, wisdom, and a deep connection to inner insights and higher truths. Individuals who embody the Seer archetype are characterized by their ability to perceive beyond the surface, gaining profound insights into the nature of reality and human experience. The Seer archetype brings a profound sense of wisdom, insight, and spiritual awareness to those who embody it. Seers may serve as guides, mentors, and sources of inspiration for others seeking a deeper understanding of themselves and the world.

Shadow side: Excessive focus on the mystical and spiritual dimensions may cause the Seer to become detached from the material and practical aspects of life, leading to a lack of grounded-ness.

Associate Archetypes

VISIONARY	HERALD
INNOVATOR	PIONEER
HISTORIAN	EXPLORER

Innate Gifts embodied

CIRCUMSPECTION	MYSTICISM
DISCERNMENT	OPTIMISM
ENTERPRISE	ORGANIZATION
INTUITION	REASSURANCE
JUSTICE	VISION

The Seer is recognized by:
- Ability to see the future with a sense of optimism.
- A prophetic mind with an understanding of the future needs of others
- A just personality with keen awareness and circumspection
- Talent for envisioning that which has not been thought of prior

What a Seer symbolizes
- Visioning & Creation
- Insights & Innovation
- Inspiration & New Paradigms
- Forecasting & Prognostication

Corresponding Cosmic Process –
VISIONING/INTUITION/SENSING/DISCERNMENT

In this process visioning precedes creation. The creation is embodied in the mind of the creator. In the cosmic sense this was symbolized as the "Word", "the Divine Mind", "God". This process precedes ALL other processes because without it there would be no material form for the manifestation of the other processes to work on. In the practical sense, this is the meditation process called "Mental Creation".

Corresponding Planetary Influence – Sun

The incarnated NATIVE of the birth chart; the will to live; vitality and the heart; authority; gold; the ruler and visionary. The life-giving principle.

Maslow's Need Correspondence – Transcendence – service to others. The pinnacle of our life's work, the state of Spiritual Equilibrium achieved. Achieving our Magnus Opus; characterized by a state of being or living that includes yet goes beyond the realm of mere material existence.

Disciplines of Seer

Arts	Governance	Media
Economics	Health	Relations
Education	Infrastructure	Science
Environment	Justice	Spirituality

Corporate Function – EXECUTIVE, MORAL & ETHICS

Legendary figures

Legend has taken numerous real people and applied the archetypal status to them, for example:

- Pythia (Oracles of Delphi)
- Sibyls
- Joseph, son of Jacob
- Nostradamus
- Edgar Cayce
- John Quigley

Egyptian Neter – Ra – *Cosmic Principle of Creation* – Ra personifies the primordial, cosmic creative impulse. Ra is the cosmic principle of creation whose visible manifestation is the Sun. All Egyptian Neteru taking part in the creation process are aspects of Ra.

SAGE

The Sage archetype is characterized by wisdom, insight, and a profound understanding of the world gained through reflection, study, judgment, and experience. Individuals who embody the Sage archetype are often sought after for their knowledge, guidance, and ability to provide clarity. The Sage sees through appearances and illusions to find the truth. The Sage archetype enriches the world with knowledge, insight, and a profound understanding of the human experience. Sages play a crucial role in guiding and enlightening others on their journeys toward personal and intellectual growth.

Shadow side: Disillusionment, detachment, and cynicism are dangers for this archetype. The weight of knowledge and the responsibility to guide others might overwhelm a Sage in their shadow, leading to stress and a sense of burden.

Associate Archetypes

SCRIBE	NETWORKER
TEACHER	JUDGE
SCOUT	GUIDE

Innate Gifts embodied

COUNSEL	PATIENCE
GENEROSITY	PRUDENCE
GENTILITY	SERENITY
INTEGRITY	TEMPERANCE
NURTURE	WISDOM

The Sage is recognized by:
- Ability to give and nurture life and provide guidance for growth
- A wise mind with a prudent and gentle approach to things
- A generous and patient personality with temperance and integrity
- Talent for developing and strengthening others to flourish

What a Sage symbolizes
- Wisdom & nurturing
- The passive maternal aspect
- Fertility and Growth
- Intuitive feelings and Emotions

Corresponding Cosmic Process –
INCARNATION/GROWTH/MULTIPLICATION/ELABORATION

Here the influence of the Sun inspires Earth with life, the result being endowed with form by the planets. The life principle enters and organizes the inert chemical elements, to produce a living creature, which is clothed with individual shape and qualities. This is the universal process of growth, multiplication, and propagation.

Corresponding Planetary Influence – Moon
The maternal instinct, passive energy, intuition, the process of growth, nurturing.

Maslow's Need Correspondence – Love/Belonging – friendship, family, intimacy. Affiliation with others; being accepted. The relationships that we develop as we determine our Function in Society and where we best fit in, our Raison De 'Tre.

Disciplines of Sage

Education	Health	Relations
Governance	Justice	Spirituality

Corporate Function - MARKETING

Legendary figures

Legend has taken numerous real people and applied the archetypal status to them, for example:

- Gautama Buddha
- Mother Mary
- King Solomon

- Queen of Sheba
- Marie Montessori
- Eva (Evita) Peron

Egyptian Neter – Isis (Aset) – *Cosmic Principle of Propagation –* *the* personification of divine maternal devotion, fidelity, and tenderness. The female creative power that brought forth all living creatures; the womb of the new Osirian life incarnated, nurtured, and regenerated.

WARRIOR

The Warrior archetype is characterized by strength, courage, and a strong sense of purpose. Individuals embodying the Warrior archetype are driven by a desire to protect, defend, and make a positive impact in the world. Warriors formulate plans and attempt to achieve them through force or guile, though they rarely betray their code of honor. The Warrior archetype plays a crucial role in societies and communities, contributing to the protection, progress, and well-being of individuals and the collective. Warriors inspire others through their actions and embody the strength and resilience needed to face life's challenges.

Shadow side: The Warrior archetype runs the risk of seeing violence, to others or oneself, as the answer to all problems.

Associate Archetypes

KNIGHT	ADVOCATE
AVENGER	GUARDIAN
REBEL	REVOLUTIONARY

Innate Gifts embodied

ATHLETICISM	FOCUS
CONSTANCY	FORTITUDE
COURAGE	PROTECTORSHIP
DEVOTION	RESOLVE
DISCIPLINE	VIGILANCE

The Warrior is recognized by:
- Ability to demonstrate focus, discipline, and courage at all times.
- A mind devoted to a love and commitment to a cause beyond self
- A resolved personality exhibiting vigilance and constancy
- Talent for protecting and defending those that can't defend themselves

What a Warrior symbolizes

- Courage and power
- Confidence and discipline
- Focus and constancy
- Strength and devotion

Corresponding Cosmic Process –
DECAY/DISINTEGRATION/DESTRUCTION/ELIMINATION

In this process, the influence of the Sun undoes the formative work of the planets, to reduce living organisms back to Earth. The life-force itself unlocks the form, enabling its constituent chemical elements to disintegrate. Pull up a living plant and expose it to the rays of the Sun: in a comparatively short time its carbon and oxygen will have been released into the air, and its nitrogen and mineral salts into the earth. All processes of burning, rusting, rotting, decay and elimination in general proceed by the same order of forces.

Corresponding Planetary Influence – Mars
Enthusiasm; aggression; war and the soldier; weapons of war. Mars is the planet that has anything to do with war. Mars rules our muscles and stamina.

Maslow's Need Addressed – Safety/Security – protection, security and stability. The realized state of Solace experienced by knowing that the society that we are a part of is operating in accord with divine law and has the "highest good" of ALL as the ultimate goal.

Disciplines of Warrior
Education	Health	Relations
Environment	Media	
Governance	Science	

Corporate Function - SALES

Legendary figures

Legend has taken numerous real people and applied the archetypal status to them, for example:

- Alexander III of Macedon
- Attila the Hun
- Hannibal
- Khalid ibn al-Walid
- Robin Hood
- Joan of Arc
- Harriet Tubman
- Nelson Mandela

Egyptian Neter – Sekhmet – *Cosmic Principle of Creative Fire* – Feminine aspect associated with both healing and disease. Sekhmet had both beneficent and maleficent aspects. War was waged under her Aegis. She inspired both reverence and fear.

SCHOLAR

The Scholar archetype is characterized by a profound love for knowledge, a thirst for learning, and a commitment to intellectual pursuits. Individuals embodying the Scholar archetype are driven by a desire to understand the world, seek truth, and contribute to the expansion of knowledge. The Scholar archetype enriches society by advancing knowledge, fostering intellectual growth, and inspiring a culture of learning. Scholars contribute to the collective wisdom of humanity, leaving a lasting impact on the way we understand and navigate the world.

Shadow side: A Scholar in their shadow aspect might become arrogant or condescending, believing their intellectual abilities make them superior to others, looking down on those they perceive as less knowledgeable.

Associate Archetypes

LIBERATOR	EVANGELIST
MEDIATOR	POLITICIAN
CATALYST	DETECTIVE

Innate Gifts embodied

CREDIBILITY	OBSERVATION
GNOSIS	ORATION
INQUIRY	REFORM
INTROSPECTION	RHETORIC
NATURE	SENSIBILITY

The Scholar is recognized by:
- Ability to convert raw data into useable knowledge.
- An inquisitive, probing, and analytical mind
- A thoughtful personality with freedom as a keynote
- A talent to inform, transform and reform

What a Scholar symbolizes
- Authority and credibility
- Ethics and immersion
- Transformation & refinement
- Passion & persistence

Corresponding Cosmic Process –
TRANSFORMATION/REFINEMENT/PURIFICATION/DIGESTION

The long-term action of life on Earth is the gradual transformation and refinement of the Earth's surface. Inorganic matter is gradually transformed to organic, organic to animal, and so on. Rocks are broken down by wind, rain and frost: the lava beds of volcanoes in 300 years become fertile vineyards. Soil becomes plant-tissue, plant-tissue the motion and sensation of animals. The natural law 'eat and be eaten' veils this upward transformation of matter, which proceeds by the third combination -Earth: Sun: Planets. Amorphous matter is worked on by the force of life and raised into form.

Corresponding Planetary Influence – Mercury

The mind, the intellect, and the respiration system and lungs, intelligence, the ability to communicate and the act of communication; the nervous system; transportation and vehicles of transportation; photography; lens and optical equipment.

Maslow's Need Addressed – Self Actualization – Realizing personal potential, self-fulfillment, seeking personal growth and peak experiences. The realization of the state of being or living whereas we are Applying our Talents towards a specific Discipline in the world where we are being effective and adding to the Quality of life.

Disciplines of Scholar

Education	Justice	Science
Governance	Media	Spirituality
Health	Relations	

Corporate Function - FINANCE

Legendary figures

Legend has taken numerous real people and applied the archetypal status to them, for example:

- Plato
- Aristotle
- Abraham Lincoln
- Marie Curie
- Abraham Maslow
- Albert Einstein
- Joseph Campbell
- Malcolm X

Egyptian Neter – Anubis (Anpu) – *Cosmic Principle of Transmutation* – Re-Creation or resurrection made manifest after many trials of shadows and darkness in the symbolic underworld or world of ego and illusions.

KING

The King archetype is a symbol of leadership, authority, and responsibility. It embodies qualities of benevolent rulership, guidance, and the ability to create a harmonious and just society. Individuals embodying the King archetype often find themselves in positions of leadership, whether in a family, community, organization, or society at large. The King archetype represents the embodiment of noble and benevolent leadership, fostering a sense of order, justice, and prosperity within the realms they oversee.

Shadow side: The King may fall into a pattern of abuse by eliminating weak or dissenting voices and thereby become a tyrant.

Associate Archetypes

HERO	SHAMAN	DIPLOMAT
PRIEST	ALCHEMIST	REFORMER

Innate Gifts embodied

EFFICIENCY	NOBILITY	SOLACE
EXCELLENCE	PACIFICATION	STABILITY
HUMANITY	RESPONSIBILITY	
INFLUENCE	SHREWDNESS	

The King is recognized for his ability to:
- See in crime the ability to heal the criminal
- See in corruption the ability to restore balance and efficiency to the system
- See in rebellion the opportunity to bring about calm, restoration, and balance
- To bring about solace, harmony, and stability

What a King symbolizes
- The Power of Thought and Willpower
- Authority and Influence
- Morals and Excellence
- Stability and Solace

Corresponding Cosmic Process –
DISEASE/REBELLION/CORRUPTION/CRIME

In this process form breaks loose from its natural subservience, and, overcoming spirit, reduces the whole to dead matter. Responding abnormally to the stimulus of a single planet, one particular organ or group of cells in a living being outgrows its function in the general harmony and assumes a dominant role. The uncontrolled proliferation of cancer cells, the exaggerated dominance or deficiency of the thyroid gland to produce neurotics or cretins, are examples in human pathology. Gradually such dominance overwhelms the unifying force of life deriving from the Sun and reduces first tissue and then the whole body to its inert constituents or earth.

Corresponding Planetary Influence – Saturn

The culmination of problems and the crystallization of mistakes; dissolution; bad judgment and selfishness; susceptibility to immorality; confusion and recklessness; death and tragedy; carelessness and harmful behavior; hatred and malice; emphasis on the personal ego.

Maslow's Need Addressed – Esteem – Self-esteem, confidence, achievement, respect of others, respect by others, responsibility. The state of gaining self-respect and admiration as a result of realizing our unique Gift & Talent which we are gifted to Serve humanity.

Disciplines of King

Economics	Health	Infrastructure
Education	Justice	
Governance	Relations	

Corporate Function – RESEARCH & DEVELOPMENT (R&D)

Legendary figures

Legend has taken numerous real people and applied the archetypal status to them, for example:

- Pharaoh Akhenaton
- King Solomon
- Cleopatra
- King Arthur
- Julius Caesar
- Henry VIII
- Queen Elizabeth I
- Queen Victoria
- Haile Selassie I
- King Louis XVI
- Mansa Musa
- Chaka Zulu

Egyptian Neter – Set – *Cosmic Principle of Materialism* – ruling principle of the material world, symbolized by chaos and disunity, multiplicity, and form. Potential forces of darkness and opposition.

SERVER

The Server archetype typically embodies qualities associated with service, support, and dedication. Individuals who align with the Server archetype often find fulfillment in helping others, offering assistance, and contributing to the well-being of their communities.

Shadow side: The server must be careful and not give up so much of their power as to be reduced to a slave.

Associate Archetypes

CLOWN	GRIOT
SAMARITAN	CAREGIVER
ANGEL	HEDONIST

Innate Gifts embodied

ALTRUISM	DIPLOMACY
BENEVOLENCE	EMPATHY
COMPASSION	ENTHUSIASM
CORDIALITY	HEALING
DEDICATION	SUPPORTIVENESS

The Servant is recognized by:
- Ability to recognize and be supportive of basic human needs.
- A compassionate mind with a genuine enthusiasm towards serving the needs of others
- A cordial personality with the embodiment of altruism
- Talent to dedicate self to a person or cause in a selfless, benevolent manner

What a Servant symbolizes
- Healing and Compassion
- Empathy and Support
- Diplomacy and Justice
- Altruism and Service

Corresponding Cosmic Process –
ADAPTATION/HEALING/RENEWAL/INVENTION

The fifth process represents the rediscovery of spirit by matter, through the mediation of right form. Inert matter, assuming with planetary help new forms suitable to changed circumstances, attracts to itself the intervention of solar forces. The working of this order is most clear in its aspect as a counteractivity to disease and crime. Healing means that the inert matters or poisons produced by the last process must be eliminated and the tissues once more rearrange themselves in their right place and form, permitting the renewed circulation of the lifeblood.

Corresponding Planetary Influence – Jupiter
The essence of healing, fulfillment, of prayers and wishes coming true; peace, success and increases; forgiveness; the selfless servant; wisdom and good judgment; the ability to overcome obstacles; faith, hope, charity, compassion, friendship. Providence; power in the benevolent sense; generosity; true genius; rewards; true love.

Maslow's Need Addressed – Physical / Physiological – Air, food, drink, shelter, warmth, sex, sleep, etc. The physical and mental state of mind derived from having discerned and determined how to meet the collective needs of the world in addition to our own individual needs.

Disciplines of Servant

| Education | Health | Relations |
| Governance | Justice | Spirituality |

Corporate Function – HUMAN RESOURCES (HR)

Legendary figures

Legend has taken numerous real people and applied the archetypal status to them, for example:

- Moses
- Jesus
- Francis of Assisi
- Florence Nightingale
- Mother Teresa
- Cesar Chavez
- Mahatma Gandhi
- Dr. Martin Luther King, Jr.

Egyptian Neter – Horus (Heru) – Cosmic Principle of Divinity Realized – Heru in Egyptian means "he who is above". The goal of all esoteric teaching, "the return to source"; the mortal god.

ARTISAN

The Artisan archetype is associated with creativity, spontaneity, and a deep appreciation for aesthetics. Individuals who embody the Artisan archetype are often driven by a desire to express themselves artistically and to bring beauty and innovation into the world.

Associate Archetypes

DIVA	ANALYST
MAGICIAN	MYSTIC
POET	ATHLETE

Innate Gifts embodied

AESTHETICS	CREATION
ARITHMETIC	GEOMETRY
ART	INDUSTRY
CHEER	MUSIC
COMPOSITION	PRECISION

The Artisan is recognized by:

- Ability to improvise novel solutions to problems and restore beauty, balance and renewal to the world
- An inner childlike emotional side intertwined with a staggering logical mind
- A cheerful personality that is magnetic in quality, the light in the room
- Talent for manifesting into reality that which has never been introduced previously

What an Artisan symbolizes

- Beauty and form
- The Creative Power of the Mind
- New Inventions
- Intelligence of the Heart

Corresponding Cosmic Process – REGENERATION/RE-CREATION/CHANGE OF NATURE/ART

In this process, form, giving order to matter, itself becomes life or spirit. The creature emulates the creator, and itself creates. Planets are but the forms or reflections of solar influence. But they too may in some way aspire to be suns, and with Jupiter and Saturn we see their transformation already far advanced. The planet, organizing the earth or matter available to it in imitation of its sun, becomes sun to its own satellites and system.

Corresponding Planetary Influence – Venus

The essence of beauty, physical and sexual attraction; affections, partnerships and weddings; money and possessions of a movable nature, sense of humor; clothing and fashion.

Maslow's Need Addressed – Aesthetics – symmetry, order, and beauty. The enrichment that we contribute to the world resulting from the "Genuine Significant Value" that we create, instill, and are guided by that ultimately adds Value to the world.

Disciplines of Artisan

Arts	Infrastructure	Relations
Education	Media	Spirituality
Environment	Science	

Corporate Function - PRODUCTION

Legendary figures

Legend has taken numerous real people and applied the archetypal status to them, for example:
- Su Song
- Archimedes
- Leonardo da Vinci
- Benjamin Franklin
- Nikola Tesla
- George Washington Carver

Egyptian Neter –Osiris (Assur) – Cosmic Principle of Regeneration – Re-Creation or resurrection made manifest after many trials of shadows and darkness in the symbolic underworld or world of ego and illusions.

7 Primary Activation Archetypes and sub-types

Societal Transformation archetypes

Seer	Sage	Warrior	Scholar	King	Server	Artisan
Visionary	Philosopher	Protector	Researcher	Ruler	Caregiver	Creator
Prophet	Mentor	Champion	Teacher	Matriarch	Healer	Builder
Mystic	Historian	Defender	Inventor	Patriarch	Helper	Craftsperson
Oracle	Judge	Hero	Librarian	Lawgiver	Advocate	Performer
Truth-teller	Hermit	Rebel	Analyst	Diplomat	Nurturer	Storyteller
Innovator	Mediator	Enforcer	Theorist	Priest	Counselor	Musician
Alchemist	Elder	Avenger	Critic	Reformer	Volunteer	Designer

Traditional, ancient, or primordial archetypes

Seer	Sage	Warrior	Scholar	King	Server	Artisan
Oracle	Guru	Knight	Scribe	Emperor	Caretaker	Craftsman
Shaman	Elder	Samurai	Alchemist	Chieftain	Healer	Builder
Sibyl	Teacher	Gladiator	Historian	Patriarch	Attendant	Smith
Mystic	Scribe	Champion	Librarian	Ruler	Guardian	Weaver
Prophet	Druid	Guardian	Philosopher	Steward	Nurturer	Potter
Augur	Savant	Defender	Teacher	Lawgiver	Helper	Poet
Diviner	Magus	Avenger	Griot	Sovereign	Acolyte	Storyteller

7-STEP FRAMEWORK DIAGRAM

The 7-Step Awaken to Your Life Purpose Framework

The Awaken to Your Life Purpose Framework is not a rigid formula, but a living process that mirrors the way creation itself unfolds. It helps you move from burnout and uncertainty into clarity, confidence, and alignment with your deepest gifts. This journey begins by awakening what has always been within you — your innate gifts and passions — and then guiding you to design a life and enterprise that expresses them fully.

The framework flows in three natural phases: rediscovery, activation, and expansion. In the rediscovery phase, you uncover your hidden gifts and passions, recognizing the spark that has always been present. In the activation phase, you align those gifts with purpose and begin building a pathway to serve others in meaningful ways. Finally, in the expansion phase, you create structures and relationships that sustain your vision, allowing your fire to scale beyond you.

Rather than treating purpose as something you must acquire from outside, the framework reveals that your destiny has always been rooted in the gifts you carry. By embracing these steps, you transition from fear and dependence on external security into the freedom of a purpose-driven life, one that transforms both your own future and the lives of those you are called to serve.

Life Destiny Map
powered by The Fire Within™

Henry Shelton   Assure Coaching

Turning Your Life Purpose into a
Heart-Centered Business

Awaken To Your Life Purpose Online Course
7 Organic Steps to Attain Purpose, Passion & Profits

		OBJECTIVE	OUTCOME	DELIVERABLE	LAW				
Find your "Aha Moment!" (Innate Gifts)	1	Identify your NATURAL BIRTH GIFTS & TALENTS.	**Accessing Your Archetypes** Finding **Clarity** to ignite the **Fire Within**	*Finding your* **Unique Essence** – (that which makes you 1 in 10 million!) *"Gifts of Archetypes"*	**The Fire Within**	DHARMA	Emanation - World of Archetypes	Your Inner Spark	**Soul's Purpose**
	2	Discover what you are PASSIONATE about by identifying the NEEDS/WANTS/PROBLEMS in the world that you are moved by your conscience to meet. (What PROBLEM are you SOLVING?)	**Discover Your Passion & Purpose Exercise** **Activation Statement*** Raison d'être **"Personal Significance"**	*Finding your* **Voice**, **Calling**, and **Soul's Code** *Finding your* **Hedgehog Concept** – (that you can become the best in the world at!)	**My Life Purpose**	LOVE	World of Creation	Emotional Involvement	
Monetize Your Passion/Purpose (Business Model)	3	Service: VALUE PROPOSITION - WHY would someone choose you to provide the solution given other choices	**"Genuine Significant Value"**	*Your Social Value Proposition*	**Value Model & Sacred Patrons**	SERVICE	World of Formation	Grounding Your Purpose	**Business Model**
	4	BUSINESS MODEL – the structure of your enterprise that will facilitate the delivery of Value to your clients Identify your "IDEAL CLIENT" OR "SACRED PATRONS"	**Business Model w/projections** Target Customer & Niche Market • Demographics • Psychographics	*Create your* **Business Model Canvas w/** *Customer Persona(s) ("Sacred Patrons")*		CREATION			
Systemize (Organize & Grow) Your Business Enterprise	5	Define Core **BUSINESS FUNCTIONS**	**Organization Chart & Customer Journey**	*Write Business Plan & Pitch Deck*	**The Million Dollar Business Plan**	FORM	World of Action	Building Your Enterprise	**Fundable Business Plan**
	6	Establish **BUSINESS PROCESSES** for each functional area.	Systems & Processes Online Sales/Marketing Campaign Lead Generation/Conversion Strategy Sessions	*Develop the Go to Market Plan*		EFFICIENCY			
	7	Develop a **WINNING TEAM** to drive the model.	Success Team Identification, Recruitment, and Plan	**Onboard Success Team**		HARMOINY			

HUMAN NEEDS LEVELS

Maslow's Hierarchy of Needs

Since I incorporated the need to assess an individual's desire to work at a particular level of the human needs' hierarchy or spectrum, I'm including this section in the appendix to introduce Maslow's hierarchy of needs with the addendum of two additional (aesthetics and transcendence) needs that I find important for achieving a holistic worldview.

This will assist individuals with understanding where they identify on the human needs' spectrum. Later in other works, I will refer to this complete set of seven needs as Henry's heterarchy of needs rather than Maslow's hierarchy of needs. I do so because unlike Maslow I feel that some needs near the top of the "hierarchy" can still be achieved without first completely fulfilling the lower needs.

As seen in the figure on the following page, Maslow's hierarchy of needs is a psychological theory proposed by Abraham Maslow in the mid-20th century. It categorizes human needs into a hierarchy, with basic physiological needs at the bottom and higher-level psychological needs at the top.

Human Needs Hierarchy Pyramid

TRADITIONAL MEANINGS		ESOTERIC RENDITION
Helping others to achieve self-actualization. (Service to Humanity!)	Transcendence	The pinnacle of our life's work, the state of Spiritual Equilibrium are achieved our **Magnus Opus**; characterized by a state of being or living that includes, yet goes beyond the realm of mere material existence
Appreciation and search for beauty, balance, form, mastery of self.	Aesthetics	The Enrichment that we contribute to the world by virtue of the "Genuine Significant Value" that we create, instill, and are guided by that ultimately adds Value to the world
Realizing personal potential, self-fulfillment, seeking personal growth and peak experiences.	Self-Actualization	The realization of the state of being or living whereas we are Applying our Talents towards a specific Discipline in the world where we are being effective and adding to the Quality of life. Finding our Raison DE'Tre (reason for being)
Self-esteem, confidence, achievement, respect of others, respect by others, responsibility;	Esteem	The state of gaining self-respect and admiration as a result of realizing our unique Gift & Talent which we are gifted to Serve humanity
Family, friendship, work group; relationships, affection, intimacy; etc.	Love / Belonging	The relationships that we develop as we determine our Function in Society and where we best fit in.
Protection from elements, security of body and resources order; law; stability; etc.	Safety / Security	The realized state of Solace experienced by knowing that the society that we are a part of is operating in accord with divine law and has the "highest good" of ALL as the ultimate goal
Air, food, drink, shelter, warmth, sex, sleep; etc.	Physical / Physiological	The physical and mental state of mind derived from having discerned and determined how to meet the collective needs of the world in addition to our own individual needs

Physical and Physiological

The physiological needs represent the foundational and most fundamental requirements for human survival and well-being. These needs include:

1. **Air**: The need for oxygen to sustain life.

2. **Water**: The need for an adequate and clean water supply.

3. **Food**: The need for nourishment and sustenance.

4. **Shelter**: The need for a safe and secure physical environment.

5. **Sleep**: The need for sufficient and quality rest.

These physiological needs are considered essential for maintaining basic bodily functions and ensuring survival. According to Maslow's theory, until these basic physiological needs are met, individuals are unlikely to focus on or be motivated by higher-level needs such as safety, social belonging, esteem, and self-actualization. Once the physiological needs are satisfied, individuals can progress to addressing higher-level needs in the hierarchy.

Safety and Security

The safety and security needs in Maslow's hierarchy represent the second level in the hierarchy, following the physiological needs. These needs are focused on creating a stable and secure environment to protect individuals from harm and ensure their well-being. The safety and security needs include:

1. **Personal Safety**: The need for physical safety and protection from potential threats or danger.

2. **Financial Security**: The need for economic stability and the assurance that basic financial requirements will be met.

3. **Health and Well-being**: The need for physical and mental health, as well as access to healthcare resources.

4. **Safety Nets**: The need for a support system, such as family or social networks, that can provide assistance in times of need.

5. **Stability and Order**: The need for a predictable and organized environment, where individuals can feel a sense of control and routine.

Meeting safety and security needs helps individuals feel a sense of stability and protection, allowing them to focus on higher-level needs such as social connections, esteem, and self-actualization. In Maslow's theory, these needs are considered crucial for overall psychological well-being and personal development.

Love and Belonging

The love/belonging need in Maslow's hierarchy represents the third level in the hierarchy, following physiological and safety needs. These needs are centered around interpersonal relationships and social connections. The love/belonging needs include:

1. **Friendship**: The need for meaningful friendships and social connections.

2. **Intimacy**: The need for close and personal relationships, including romantic relationships.

3. **Family**: The need for a sense of belonging within a family or other close-knit social groups.

4. **Social Acceptance**: The need to be accepted by peers and the larger community.

5. **Affection and Love**: The need to give and receive love, both emotionally and physically.

Fulfilling these love and love/belonging needs contributes to a sense of connection, acceptance, and support. According to Maslow, when individuals have satisfied their physiological and safety needs, they seek to satisfy these social needs, forming relationships and bonds with others. Meeting these needs is crucial for overall emotional well-being and the development of a positive self-concept.

Self-Esteem

Self-esteem needs in Maslow's hierarchy represent the fourth level in the hierarchy, following physiological, safety, and love and belongingness needs. These needs are focused on building a positive self-image and gaining recognition and respect from others. The self-esteem needs include:

1. **Achievement**: The need for a sense of accomplishment and success in personal and professional endeavors.

2. **Recognition**: The need for acknowledgment, appreciation, and validation from others.

3. **Self-Worth**: The need to feel valuable and worthy as an individual.

4. **Competence**: The need to demonstrate competence and effectiveness in various activities.

5. **Independence**: The need for autonomy and the ability to make decisions independently.

Fulfilling these self-esteem needs contributes to a sense of confidence, competence, and a positive evaluation of oneself. According to Maslow's theory, individuals strive to achieve these needs after satisfying lower-level needs, seeking to build a strong sense of self and gain the esteem and recognition of others. Meeting these needs is essential for developing healthy self-esteem and a positive self-concept.

Self-actualization

The self-actualization need in Maslow's hierarchy represents the highest level in the hierarchy, following physiological, safety, love/belonging, and self-esteem needs. These needs are focused on personal growth, realizing one's potential, and achieving a sense of fulfillment. The self-actualization needs include:

1. **Creativity**: The need for expressing creativity and engaging in activities that foster innovation and originality.

2. **Problem Solving**: The need to tackle challenges, solve problems, and engage in meaningful intellectual pursuits.

3. **Self-Reflection**: The need for introspection and a deeper understanding of oneself.

4. **Morality and Ethics**: The need to adhere to personal values, ethics, and a sense of morality.

5. **Autonomy**: The need for self-direction and the ability to make choices aligned with one's values.

6. **Acceptance of Facts and Realities**: The need to accept the facts of life and the realities of oneself, others, and the world.

Fulfilling these self-actualization needs involves a continuous process of personal development and striving for personal potential. According to Maslow, only a small percentage of individuals reach this level of need fulfillment, as it requires a strong foundation of satisfaction in the lower-level needs. Achieving self-actualization leads to a profound sense of purpose, authenticity, and a meaningful life.

Aesthetics

It's important to note that Abraham Maslow did not explicitly include a category for aesthetics in his original hierarchy of needs. However, some interpretations and adaptations of his theory, as well as subsequent research, have considered aesthetic needs as part of the self-actualization level or as a separate category. With that in mind, here's an interpretation that includes aesthetics:

Aesthetic Needs within Self-Actualization: Aesthetic needs encompass the appreciation of beauty, harmony, and creativity. While not explicitly outlined by Maslow, they are often considered part of the self-actualization level, representing a desire for experiences that evoke a sense of beauty and transcendence. Aesthetic needs may include:

1. **Appreciation of Art and Beauty**: The need to engage with and create art, whether visual, auditory, or otherwise.

2. **Connection with Nature**: The need to be in natural environments and appreciate the beauty of the natural world.

3. **Cultural and Intellectual Stimulation**: The need for exposure to diverse cultural experiences, intellectual challenges, and stimulating ideas.

4. **Cultural Expression:** The need for engaging in and appreciating various forms of cultural expression, including music, dance, literature, and other artistic endeavors that contribute to a sense of aesthetic pleasure and cultural richness.

5. **Environmental Harmony:** The need for creating or being in environments that are aesthetically pleasing,

harmonious, and visually appealing, contributing to a sense of well-being and a connection between individuals and their surroundings.

Fulfilling aesthetic needs can contribute to a deeper sense of meaning and enrichment in life. While not explicitly outlined by Maslow, the pursuit of aesthetic experiences is often seen as a component of self-actualization, reflecting an individual's quest for personal growth, beauty, and the transcendent aspects of human experience.

Transcendence

Transcendence needs, also known as self-transcendence, is a concept that was added later by Maslow to his original hierarchy. Transcendence represents the desire to go beyond self and contribute to something beyond personal fulfillment. This level extends beyond self-actualization and includes a focus on the greater good and a connection to something larger than oneself. Transcendence needs include:

1. **Altruism**: The need to engage in acts of kindness and altruistic behaviors for the well-being of others.

2. **Spirituality**: The need for spiritual experiences, connection with something greater, and a sense of meaning and purpose.

3. **Service to Others**: The need to contribute to the welfare and happiness of others, often through acts of service or mentorship.

4. **Ecological Awareness**: The need to connect with and care for the environment and the broader ecosystem.

5. **Global Unity**: The need to feel connected to humanity as a whole and work towards the betterment of society.

Fulfilling transcendence needs involves a shift from individual concerns to a broader, collective perspective. Maslow suggested that individuals who reach this level experience a deep sense of fulfillment by contributing to the well-being of others and connecting with a purpose beyond personal goals. It's important to note that while transcendence needs were proposed by Maslow, they are not always included in every interpretation of his hierarchy.

INDUSTRY SECTORS ANALYSIS

THE 12 DISCIPLINES (SECTORS OF SOCIETY)

In the pursuit of a life that is both fulfilling and impactful, it becomes essential to align our personal ambitions with the broader currents that shape society. As we navigate the complexities of modern life, it is easy to become ensnared by routines or career paths that serve neither our highest potential nor the collective good. This chapter invites you to explore your life purpose within the context of societal transformation, offering a roadmap to discover a career path that not only ignites your passion but also contributes to the evolution of our shared world.

Drawing from the principles of systems theory and the philosophy of science, this exploration is rooted in the understanding that every aspect of society is interconnected. The arts, economics, education, and other disciplines discussed herein are not isolated silos but are part of a dynamic, evolving system. By recognizing the role that these domains play in shaping our world, you can gain clarity on how your unique gifts and talents can be directed toward a meaningful and impactful career. This chapter serves as a guide to help you identify where your passions intersect with the needs of society, offering you the opportunity to be both an architect of your destiny and a catalyst for positive change.

Listed below are 12 areas of society factored into the "Accessing Your Archetype" assessment instrument that are idea disciplines to focus on for societal transformation. Included with the description of each are also listed the:

- vision for societal transformation that aligns with evolutionary consciousness,
- the dangers of the current state of that discipline,
- and lastly the afforded opportunities to improve that discipline to aid in creating a better society and world.

1. Arts

Description: The arts encompass creative expression through various forms such as visual arts, music, theater, literature, and dance. They reflect and shape cultural values, influence social norms, and provide a medium for individual and collective expression.

- **Vision:** The arts will become a powerful tool for awakening collective consciousness, fostering empathy, and bridging cultural divides. By promoting inclusivity and diversity, the arts can inspire societal transformation, encouraging creativity that aligns with the evolution of human consciousness.

- **Dangers:** The current state of the arts is often commercialized, with creativity stifled by profit motives and mainstream trends. There is also a risk of cultural homogenization, where unique artistic expressions are marginalized.

- **Opportunities:** Encouraging support for independent artists, promoting art education, and fostering community-based art initiatives can revitalize the arts. Leveraging digital platforms to share diverse artistic expressions globally can also drive societal transformation.

2. Economics

Description: Economics involves the production, distribution, and consumption of goods and services. It encompasses systems of trade, financial markets, and the management of resources, impacting every aspect of society.

- **Vision:** Economics will evolve into a system that values sustainability, equity, and well-being over mere profit. A regenerative economy will focus on long-term prosperity, reducing inequality and ensuring that economic activities enhance the health of the planet and its inhabitants.

- **Dangers:** The current economic model prioritizes short-term gains, leading to resource depletion, environmental degradation, and social inequality. The focus on GDP as a sole measure of success overlooks the well-being of people and the planet.

- **Opportunities:** Embracing circular and regenerative economic models, promoting fair trade, and developing metrics that account for environmental and social well-being can transform economics. Supporting local economies and ethical business practices can also foster a more equitable and sustainable society.

3. Education

Description: Education is the process of acquiring knowledge, skills, and values. It is a cornerstone of societal development, shaping individuals' abilities to contribute to their communities and the world at large.

- **Vision:** Education will shift towards a holistic approach that nurtures not just intellectual, but also emotional, spiritual, and social intelligence. An education system aligned with evolutionary consciousness will empower individuals to become conscious global citizens, capable of creative and critical thinking.

- **Dangers:** The current education system is often rigid, focused on rote learning and standardized testing, which can stifle creativity and critical thinking. It may also perpetuate existing social inequalities by limiting access to quality education for marginalized groups.

- **Opportunities:** Integrating holistic and experiential learning methods, promoting lifelong learning, and ensuring equitable access to education can transform this discipline. Emphasizing values such as collaboration, empathy, and global awareness will prepare future generations for the challenges of the 21st century.

4. Environment

Description: The environment refers to the natural world, including ecosystems, wildlife, and natural resources. It is the foundation of life, providing the resources needed for survival and well-being.

- **Vision:** A society that recognizes the interdependence between humans and the natural world, adopting practices that restore and protect the environment. Evolutionary consciousness will lead to a deep respect for nature, with sustainable living as the norm.

- **Dangers:** Current environmental degradation, driven by unsustainable practices such as deforestation, pollution, and overconsumption, threatens the planet's ecosystems and human survival.

- **Opportunities:** Embracing renewable energy, sustainable agriculture, and conservation efforts can protect and restore the environment. Educating people about their impact on the planet and encouraging eco-friendly practices can also lead to significant positive change.

5. Governance

Description: Governance refers to the systems and processes by which societies are managed, including laws, policies, and institutions. It is crucial for maintaining order, protecting rights, and ensuring justice.

- **Vision:** Governance will evolve to be more inclusive, transparent, and participatory, with a focus on serving the common good. Leaders will be guided by principles of fairness, integrity, and responsibility, aligning policies with the well-being of all citizens and the planet.

- **Dangers:** Current governance structures can be plagued by corruption, inequality, and inefficiency. The concentration of power in the hands of a few often leads to decisions that benefit the privileged at the expense of the majority.

- **Opportunities:** Implementing participatory democracy, promoting transparency, and strengthening institutions can improve governance. Encouraging civic engagement and holding leaders accountable will ensure that governance aligns with the needs of society and the environment.

6. Health

Description: Health encompasses physical, mental, and emotional well-being. It is influenced by factors such as access to medical care, nutrition, lifestyle, and environmental conditions.

- **Vision:** Health will be redefined to include a holistic approach that integrates mind, body, and spirit. Society will prioritize preventive care, mental health, and well-being, with healthcare systems that are accessible, affordable, and focused on the whole person.

- **Dangers:** The current healthcare system is often reactive rather than preventive, focusing on treating illness rather than promoting overall well-being. There is also a significant disparity in access to quality healthcare, particularly in underserved communities.

- **Opportunities:** Promoting preventive care, mental health awareness, and holistic health practices can transform healthcare. Ensuring equitable access to healthcare and integrating traditional and modern medicine can improve health outcomes for all.

7. Infrastructure

Description: Infrastructure refers to the physical and organizational structures essential for the operation of society, including transportation, communication, energy, and water systems. This also includes the repair and modernization of outdated and insufficiently maintained infrastructure, such as bridges and highways, that may pose safety risks.

- **Vision:** Infrastructure will be designed with sustainability, resilience, and inclusivity in mind. Smart cities and green infrastructure will support a high quality of life, with systems that are efficient, adaptable, environmentally friendly, and safe. The restoration of aging bridges, highways, and other transportation networks will prioritize safety and durability, ensuring that all structures meet modern standards.

- **Dangers:** Current infrastructure can be outdated, inefficient, and dangerous, particularly in the case of older bridges and highways that were not built to handle today's traffic volume and size. Poor maintenance, reliance on fossil fuels, and hazardous urban planning pose significant risks to public safety and the environment. Tragically, the loss of lives, such as when my brother ventured onto a narrow bridge that could not safely accommodate two large vehicles, highlights the dire need for urgent infrastructure repair.

- **Opportunities:** Investing in the repair and modernization of old bridges and highways, alongside renewable energy, sustainable transportation, and resilient infrastructure, can greatly enhance public safety and environmental sustainability. By promoting green building practices and leveraging technology to create smart, adaptable infrastructure, society can be transformed for the better—mitigating future accidents and improving overall quality of life.

8. Justice

Description: Justice involves the legal and moral principles that govern fairness, equality, and the protection of rights within society. It is foundational to maintain social order and protecting human dignity.

- **Vision:** A just society will be one where equality, fairness, and human rights are upheld for all. The justice system will be transformed to be more restorative than punitive, focusing on healing and reconciliation rather than retribution.

- **Dangers:** The current justice system can be biased, with systemic inequalities that disproportionately affect marginalized communities. The focus on punishment rather than rehabilitation often leads to cycles of violence and incarceration.

- **Opportunities:** Reforming the justice system to focus on restorative justice, ensuring equal access to legal resources, and addressing systemic inequalities can lead to a more just and equitable society. Promoting human rights and social justice at all levels can foster a culture of fairness and compassion.

9. Media

Description: Media refers to the channels of communication through which information is disseminated to the public, including television, radio, newspapers, and digital platforms. It plays a crucial role in shaping public opinion and culture.

- **Vision:** Media will evolve to be a force for truth, education, and positive social change. Aligned with evolutionary consciousness, media will promote diverse voices, critical thinking, and constructive dialogue, empowering citizens to make informed decisions.

- **Dangers:** The current media landscape can be dominated by sensationalism, misinformation, and polarization. The concentration of media ownership can limit diverse perspectives, while the pursuit of profit often overshadows ethical journalism.

- **Opportunities:** Supporting independent and ethical journalism, promoting media literacy, and encouraging diverse content creation can improve the media landscape. Leveraging media to highlight positive stories and solutions can also contribute to societal transformation.

10. Relationships

Description: Relationships refer to the connections between individuals, families, communities, and nations. They are foundational to social cohesion and well-being.

- **Vision:** Relationships will be based on mutual respect, understanding, and collaboration. In a society aligned with evolutionary consciousness, interpersonal and collective relationships will foster empathy, compassion, and a sense of interconnectedness.

- **Dangers:** The current state of relationships can be strained by individualism, inequality, and social fragmentation. The erosion of community bonds and the rise of divisiveness can lead to social isolation and conflict.

- **Opportunities:** Promoting communication, conflict resolution, and community-building initiatives can strengthen relationships. Encouraging practices that foster empathy and connection, such as cooperative living and cross-cultural exchange, can enhance social harmony.

11. Science

Description: Science involves the systematic study of the natural world through observation and experimentation. It drives technological advancement and shapes our understanding of the universe.

- **Vision:** Science will be guided by ethical principles and a commitment to the well-being of all life. In alignment with evolutionary consciousness, scientific inquiry will focus on solutions that enhance sustainability, health, and harmony with the natural world.

- **Dangers:** The current scientific paradigm can be overly focused on materialism, sometimes ignoring ethical considerations and the interconnectedness of life. The pursuit of profit or power can lead to harmful technological advancements.

- **Opportunities:** Integrating ethics and holistic thinking into scientific research, promoting interdisciplinary collaboration, and focusing on sustainable and life-affirming technologies can transform science. Encouraging public engagement with science can also foster a more informed and empowered society.

12. Spirituality

Description: Spirituality refers to the search for meaning, purpose, and connection with something greater than oneself. It encompasses various beliefs, practices, and experiences that contribute to an individual's inner growth and understanding of life.

- **Vision:** Spirituality will become a guiding force in societal transformation, promoting values of love, compassion, and unity. A spiritually awakened society will recognize the interconnectedness of all life and prioritize the common good over individual gain.

- **Dangers:** The current state of spirituality can be fragmented, with materialism, dogma, and extremism often overshadowing genuine spiritual growth. The commercialization of spirituality can also dilute its true essence.

- **Opportunities:** Encouraging interfaith dialogue, promoting practices that foster inner peace and compassion, and integrating spiritual principles into daily life can enhance spirituality. Supporting spiritual education and community-based spiritual practices can also contribute to societal transformation.

Conclusion

As we draw this section to a close, it is important to recognize that the journey to discovering your life purpose is not just an individual endeavor; it is a collective one. The vision for societal transformation outlined here is a call to action, urging each of us to consider how our personal growth and career choices can contribute to a more just, sustainable, and compassionate world. Whether through the arts, science, governance, or any other discipline, the opportunities for impact are vast and varied.

Ultimately, the path you choose should resonate with your inner calling and align with the larger evolutionary consciousness that seeks to elevate humanity. In finding this alignment, you not only fulfill your highest potential but also contribute to the well-being of others and the planet. Let this section be a source of inspiration and guidance as you embark on the profound journey of living a life of purpose, passion, and transformative impact.

To begin this journey of finding your voice and discovering your life's purpose, visit our website (https://henryshelton.com/product/accessing-your-archetypes-assessment/) and take the "Accessing Your Archetypes" assessment. This assessment is designed to help you identify your dominant archetypes and provide personalized insights into your strengths, motivations, and how they can guide you toward a more fulfilling and purpose-driven life. After completing the assessment, you'll gain clarity, confidence, and courage to pursue your endeavors. For further insight, (**ONLY AFTER TAKING THE ASSESSMENT**) consider scheduling a one-on-one consultation at henryshelton.com/consultation, where you will receive personal guidance in applying this knowledge to your unique circumstances and aspirations.

Take the first step today and unlock the path to living your true purpose with clarity, confidence, and courage.

ABOUT THE AUTHOR

Henry Shelton - Transformational Speaker & Executive Coach
CEO - Assure Coaching | Founder – Soul's Code Ventures

Henry Shelton is an accomplished executive coach, speaker, author, and transformational leader, dedicated to helping individuals unlock their highest potential and align their careers with their authentic purpose. As the founder of Assure Coaching, Henry specializes in empowering corporate professionals to transition from burnout to purpose-driven entrepreneurship. His expertise lies in guiding leaders to discover and unlock their innate and natural gifts and talents, enabling them to build businesses that reflect their true calling.

With a strong background in both corporate leadership and spiritual development, Henry brings a unique approach to coaching, blending practical strategies with a deep understanding of human potential. His work through Assure Coaching focuses on helping mid to upper-level professionals exit the corporate world, leveraging their innate talents to create "heart-centered", impact driven enterprises that are not only profitable but deeply meaningful.

Henry's coaching framework includes baseline assessments that go beyond the surface, uncovering hidden abilities that often lie dormant in professionals who have been conditioned to follow traditional career paths. His clients, through his support, coaching, and mentorship, rediscover their authentic selves and chart new paths that align with their passions and purpose.

In addition to his coaching work with Assure Coaching, Henry serves as a senior leader at Soul's Code Ventures, where he applies his strategic vision and leadership experience to grow this emerging ecosystem. His combined work across both platforms has positioned him as a trusted authority in personal development, leadership transformation, and purpose-driven entrepreneurship.

Henry is passionate about speaking to audiences on topics of Life Purpose, Getting Clarity, Developing Confidence, Developing Courage, and reaching their highest potential. His message resonates deeply with those seeking to find greater fulfillment, balance, and success in both their professional and personal lives. He has inspired countless professionals to embrace their unique potential and take bold steps toward building the lives they were meant to live.